Paradise Lost

Open Guides to Literature

Series Editor: Graham Martin (Professor of Literature, The Open University)

Paradise loſt.

A
POEM

Written in
TEN BOOKS

By *JOHN MILTON*.

Licenſed and Entred according
to Order.

LONDON
Printed, and are to be ſold by *Peter Parker*
under *Creed* Church neer *Aldgate* ; And by
Robert Boulter at the *Turks Head* in *Biſhopſgate-ſtreet* ;
And *Matthias Walker*, under St. *Dunſtons* Church.
in *Fleet-ſtreet*, 1 6 6 7.

RICHARD BRADFORD

Paradise Lost

Open University Press
Buckingham · Philadelphia

Open University Press
Celtic Court
22 Ballmoor
Buckingham
MK18 1XW

and
1900 Frost Road, Suite 101
Bristol, PA 19007, USA

First Published 1992

A catalogue record of this book is available
from the British Library

Library of Congress Cataloging-in-Publication Data
Bradford, Richard, 1958–
    Paradise lost / Richard Bradford.
      p. cm. – (Open guides to literature)
    Includes bibliographical references and index.
    ISBN 0-335-09983-1 – ISBN 0-335-09982-3 (pbk.)
     1. Milton, John, 1608–1674. Paradise lost. I. Milton, John,
1608–1674. Paradise lost. II. Title. III. Series.
PR3562.B67   1992
821'.4–dc20   91-46206
                                               CIP

Typeset by Best-set Typesetter Ltd., Hong Kong
Printed in Great Britain by St Edmundsbury Press Limited
Bury St Edmunds, Suffolk

To Louie, Bill and Jan

Contents

Series Editor's Preface

The intention of this series is to provide short introductory books about major writers, texts, and literary concepts for students of courses in Higher Education which substantially or wholly involve the study of Literature.

The series adopts a pedagogic approach and style similar to that of Open University material for Literature courses. *Open Guides* aim to inculcate the reading 'skills' which many introductory books in the field tend, mistakenly, to assume that the reader already possesses. They are, in this sense, 'teacherly' texts, planned and written in a manner which will develop in the reader the confidence to undertake further independent study of the topic. They are 'open' in two senses. First, they offer a three-way tutorial exchange between the writer of the *Guide*, the text or texts in question, and the reader. They invite readers to join in an exploratory discussion of texts, concentrating on their key aspects and on the main problems which readers, coming to the texts for the first time, are likely to encounter. The flow of a *Guide* 'discourse' is established by putting questions for the reader to follow up in a tentative and searching spirit, guided by the writer's comments, but not dominated by an over-arching and single-mindedly-pursued argument or evaluation, which itself requires to be 'read'.

Guides are also 'open' in a second sense. They assume that literary texts are 'plural', that there is no end to interpretation, and that it is for the reader to undertake the pleasurable task of discovering meaning and value in such texts. *Guides* seek to provide, in compact form, such relevant biographical, historical and cultural information as bears upon the reading of the text, and they point the reader to a selection of the best available critical discussions of it. They are not in themselves concerned to propose, or to counter, particular readings of the texts, but rather to put *Guide* readers in a position to do that for themselves. Experienced travellers learn to dispense with guides, and so it should be for readers of this series.

Graham Martin

Acknowledgements

This book is intended to provide a fruitful encounter between Milton's poem, its critics and the reader, and I am grateful to the English Department, Trinity College, Dublin, for first giving me the opportunity to experiment with its undergraduates. Particular thanks are due to Nicholas Grene, Terence Brown and Geraldene Mangan. I am grateful also to the British Academy and the Humanities Faculty, University of Ulster for providing me with the funds and time to finish the book. Permission has been granted by the British Library to reprint the title page from the 1667 first edition of *Paradise Lost* and from Princeton University Library to reprint Dolle's engraving from the 1674 edition. Oxford University Press has kindly allowed me to quote from section XIX of D.J. Enright's 'Paradise Illustrated. A Sequence' (1978).

Graham Martin has been a consistently encouraging and tolerant editor, and in various ways the following people have enabled me to complete and enjoy the project: Louie and Bill Bradford, Robert Welch and Jan Elliott.

1. Introduction: Milton, the Poem and the Context

For the substance of this book our attention will shift between three points: you, me and *Paradise Lost*. I have written the *Guide* but I've not tried to tell you the 'correct' way to understand or to respond to Milton's poem. I suggest possibilities, alternative solutions to the question of 'what did Milton mean?', and I ask us to look at how different critics have come up with very different answers to this question. Chapters 2–4 follow the chronology of the poem and are designed to accompany your journey through it. For example, in Chapter 2 I assume that you won't be familiar with what happens in Books V–XII, but by Chapter 4 our discussions will allow us to draw on a more confident awareness of what Milton is trying to do and of the problems he faced in concluding his narrative. In Chapter 5 we will test our own perceptions and judgements against a more detailed survey of the poem's critics. But before we begin this journey there are several problems to be considered.

With most literary texts written between the eighteenth and twentieth centuries we can identify a sliding scale that measures the relation between what we understand from the novel or the poem and what we already know about its author and the social–historical circumstances of its composition. By sliding scale I mean that, although the poems of Seamus Heaney and W.B. Yeats or the novels of D.H. Lawrence and George Orwell will engage with the language, the politics, the social codes and the existential problems of what we might call living memory, with authors such as Swift, or even Dickens, we need to reconstruct an awareness of the context in which the text was written and understood. With Milton such an exercise in reconstruction is, in my opinion, both more difficult and problematic. Why? Because we know more about Milton's life, his literary enterprises, his marriages, his political activities and allegiances and his religious beliefs than we do about any other pre-eighteenth century English writer. The problems arise in how to deal with this knowledge. When we claim that a reading of Orwell's *1984* demands an awareness of the post-World War II global division, we are able to assume that communism, Stalinism and dictatorship are familiar and debatable concepts, but when we claim that *Paradise Lost* demands a similar awareness of Milton's involvement in the civil war, and his work as a civil servant and propagandist for the Cromwellian republic, we begin to touch upon areas of history and politics that are both unfamiliar and extremely debatable. So the three-party exchange between you, me and the poem will be interrupted by broader considerations of its context. These will occur when and where the narrative requires. For instance, Chapter 2 will deal with Milton's presentation of Satan, his fallen crew and the construction of hell. This could be interpreted as a political allegory – Satan has been associated with both Charles I and Cromwell – so we will then open the three-party exchange to historians and critics who have attempted to explain the relation between the poem, its author and their historical–political context. But it would be unwise for us to go blindly into an encounter with the shifting relations between poem, poet and context without taking with us an, admittedly rough, idea of who Milton was and of how his experiences would have affected him in writing a poem on the origins of the human race.

In what follows I shall offer a short essay on how Milton's life and his experience of seventeenth-century politics relate to *Paradise Lost*. I will direct you towards specific points of contact between the poet's life, the poem and the broader historical context, but I won't offer solutions to the questions that these raise. They will be returned to in our reading of the poem.

John Milton was born in Bread Street, London in 1608, the son of a relatively well-off scrivener, a profession which combined the functions of notary and banker. He was educated at St Paul's School, London (1620–25), and admitted to Christ's College, Cambridge in 1625. He took his BA degree in 1629 and his MA in 1632, after which he retired for five years to his father's estate in Horton, Buckinghamshire, to study classical literature and philosophy, modern mathematics and music and to continue writing poetry. In 1638 he set out on a European tour, during which he met, amongst others, Grotius and Galileo. His proposed visit to Greece was cancelled on his receiving news of the outbreak of civil war in England. He returned to London in 1639, and was later to recall: 'I thought it shameful, while my countrymen were fighting for their liberty at home, that I should be peacefully travelling for culture.' The terms 'my countrymen' and 'their liberty' indicate that his political allegiances were, at thirty, as well established and as significant as his dedication to 'culture'. These allegiances relate closely to his social and family background. He came from the relatively new mercantile and landowning class that had risen to prominence during the sixteenth century and had effectively driven a wedge into the aristocratic hierarchy. It was from this social group that the parliamentarian party of the civil war were to draw some of their most influential theorists, soldiers and politicians. From 1639 until 1659 Milton's career as a poet was secondary to his work first as a propagandist and pamphleteer for the parliamentarian cause and then as a senior civil servant to the post-civil war Cromwellian cabinet (he was appointed Secretary of Foreign Tongues to the Council of State in 1649). In 1659, just prior to the Restoration of the monarchy in 1660, Parliament took steps to have Milton arrested as a supporter of the execution of Charles I. His books were publicly burned. He was saved from punishment largely by the pleas of his friend and fellow poet Andrew Marvell, and, from 1660 until his death in 1674, he lived from teaching and from the sales of his poetic writing. *Paradise Lost* was written between 1660–65 and published in 1667 as a poem in ten books. Its restructuring to twelve books occurred in the second edition of 1674. These are the facts. How will they affect our understanding of *Paradise Lost*?

Paradise Lost is a poetic rewriting of the book of Genesis. It tells the story of the fall of Satan and his compatriots, the creation of man, and most significantly, of man's act of disobedience and its consequences. It is a literary text that goes beyond the traditional limitations of literary storytelling, because for the Christian reader this story is the first, and what happens in it will determine everything that man will subsequently be and do. The question we have to ask is to what extent the biblical narrative is transposed with seventeenth-century history and more specifically with the feelings, allegiances, prejudices and disappointments of John Milton? The most obvious correspondence between text and context will be found in the relation between Milton's religious beliefs and his political allegiances. At Cambridge he witnessed what he regarded as the inherent corruption of the Established Church (see *Lycidas*) and eventually rejected a career in the Church of England. He began to sympathize more and more with the Puritan, Calvinist tradition whose literal interpretation of scripture as a guide to the social and political organization formed the theoretical basis for the parliamentary party in the civil war, and, more significantly, became the dominant political and religious code of the post-war Cromwellian Protectorate. In our reading of the poem we should bear the following questions in mind. The Cromwellian republic was regarded by its founders and administrators as biblical doctrine in political and social practice – a kind of substitute for the earthly paradise enjoyed by man before the Fall. It failed. Can we therefore assume that *Paradise Lost* was intended to tell two stories of the Fall? To what extent did Milton's own experience of the cataclysmic events of 1640–60 prompt him to transpose contemporary events with the biblical story of our origins? Was his own faith and certainty in Christian doctrine – which this story encodes – challenged or compromised by his experience of men responding to what they believed was the will of God and in so doing bringing about political division and massive loss of life? And finally, what purpose did Milton hope to serve in inviting his contemporaries to look again at the story of their origins and perhaps to re-examine their perceptions of good and evil?

In considering these questions we will be continually reminded that *Paradise Lost* is a literary text. With non-literary texts such as political pamphlets, letters or journals there is a reasonably clear division between what the author says about his world and what for us are the known facts and circumstances that surround his comments and observations. But literature creates its own world, sets up its own fictional characters, circumstances and chains of events. These might resemble or conflict with the world and the experiences of the author, but we will always find ourselves shifting uneasily between the known and the created. *Paradise Lost* sends this already unstable equation into a bewildering cycle of tensions and questions. First of all its characters are both fictional and real. They are fictional in the sense that Milton creates the linguistic patterns within which they present themselves to us and to one another, but they are real in the sense that God, Satan, Adam and Eve inhabit texts, circumstances and codes of belief beyond the poem. Now the complications begin to set in. If we are not Christian believers, they are not real characters; both the Bible and the poem are literary texts. Does this mean that we should judge them in the way that we judge other literary characters (is God, like King Lear, a tragic old fool?); or should we simply respect them as inhabitants of a particular socio-cultural code, rather like the figures in classical, Hindu or Islamic tales and epics? Further complications emerge when we begin to suspect that the resemblances between the Satanic rebellion, the creation and fall of man and the history of mid-seventeenth-century England are not accidental. Irrespective of whether we believe in God or Satan, the characters who carry these titles in Milton's poem bear a curious resemblance to figures such as Charles I and Cromwell, whose existence is beyond question.

As we shall see, the tension between the created and the known reaches far beyond the modern division between Christian and non-Christian readers. For instance the fact that Eve initiated the Fall is not challenged by Milton, but was his rewriting of these events in any way affected by his own attitude to women? His marriage to Mary Powell in 1642 was a disaster and their separation was conveniently provided by her family's Royalist allegiances. His pro-divorce pamphlet *The Doctrine and Discipline of Divorce* was published in 1643. We have the facts, but, as we shall see, any judgement on whether Milton's experiences influenced his presentation of the female prototype will be determined as much by what we find in the poem as by what we know about the poet. Indeed, there is not a single point of religious, political, aesthetic, sexual or psychological controversy that has not divided interpreters of the poem in the three centuries since its publication, and these divisions are created not by interpretations of the facts but by how the poem itself can cause us to think again about the stability of facts, truth and certainty.

Some details about how to use the *Guide*. The bibliography will include publication details of every text referred to in the study. If I refer to surname or surname and page number, the source will be found in the bibliography. There are a number of modern editions of *Paradise Lost*, but the best, with the most detailed editorial notes particularly on its classical and biblical correspondences, is the Longman (edited by Alastair Fowler, 1968). For Milton's other poetic writing use the Longman *Complete Shorter Poems* (edited by John Carey, 1968). All references to Milton's prose works are from the *Complete Prose Works of John Milton* (edited by D.M. Wolfe *et al.*, Yale University Press, 1953). This will be referred to as 'Yale'.

2. Openings: Books I–IV

There are three openings to *Paradise Lost*: Marvell's prefatory poem; Milton's note on 'The Verse'; and the first twenty-six lines of Book I in which Milton introduces the reader to the subject of the poem and seeks the assistance of the 'Heavenly Muse' in his creative task.

Superficially these three sections do not seem to have a great deal in common, but let us assume that Milton was fully aware of the effect that openings – prefaces, dedications, explanatory notes – have on the reader. It is a new text, a new experience. We are uncertain of what is to come and we are searching for a context, a frame of reference, which might prepare us for what follows. So, before considering Book I as a whole, let us examine these sections in detail and see if there are threads of meaning that we can draw together; issues and questions that Milton intends to stay in the mind of the reader in our journey through the twelve books.

Read the first twenty-six lines and consider the following questions: Why does Milton maintain an uncertain balance between informing the reader of his intention and, at the same time, seeking the assistance of the 'Heavenly Muse'? Could it be that he acknowledges the subject of his poem as too vast and fundamental to be dealt with by a mere mortal writer? If so, is he politely deferring to religious authority or subtly claiming that only John Milton is equipped to 'assert external providence,/And justify the ways of God to men'?

DISCUSSION

Understanding seventeenth-century writings is a two dimensional process. First we can settle our most immediate uncertainties by referring to the annotations and footnotes provided by modern editions. Second we can engage with interpretive problems which are at once accessible and problematic. In the former case 'Oreb', 'Sinai', 'Sion Hill', 'Siloa's Brook' and the 'Heavenly Muse' are all explained in Alastair Fowler's edition as details of the poem's invocation of classical and biblical contexts, the three major sources for the poem being the classical epics of Homer and Virgil and the Old Testament. But it might be more productive to look for problems of interpretation that cannot simply be resolved by footnotes and readers' guides. What paradoxes and interpretive uncertainties can we find that will trouble the reader, irrespective of that person's familiarity with literary convention and seventeenth-century vocabulary? One line seems to me to be particularly odd. Milton claims to be pursuing 'things unattempted yet in prose or rhyme' (16). This appears to be an announcement of the originality of the project, but it also incorporates a contradiction in terms. How can Milton claim to be writing a narrative poem about 'things unattempted' when they constitute the substance of the Old Testament and, particularly for the seventeenth-century reader, form the accepted and unchallenged story of the beginning of the human race? To tackle this paradox we should consider a basic question about *Paradise Lost*: What is it? It is a poem and, to broaden the context, a literary text. From this we might reinterpret Milton's line as 'things unattempted yet in English literature'. This would make sense because although biblical themes, narratives and images had been used and addressed in literary writing, no one had attempted to transplant the substance of the Old Testament, along with its attendant theological problems, into a single literary text.

This raises an even more complex question. If the story were already known, and indeed regarded as an indisputable truth, what were Milton's objectives in telling it again? Look at lines 25 and 26; 'I may assert external providence,/And justify the ways of God to men'. He seems to claim that by placing the unquestioned truths of Christianity at the mercy of the emotive immediacies of literary writing, he will supplement biblical doctrine with a higher degree of certainty and clarity. Our judgement of his success in an enterprise of such magnitude will depend on our own beliefs and, even if we suspend these a priori conditions, upon our perception of the poem as a whole. The difficulties attendent upon this judgement will intensify as we move through the poem, but for the moment let us gather more evidence from the opening. **Now read Marvell's prefatory poem and the note on 'The Verse' keeping in mind the uncertain relation between literature and Christian belief. What attitude towards the subject does the poem convey?**

DISCUSSION

Marvell's poem seems to me to strike an anxious, apologetic note. Consider the following lines (5–12):

> Heaven, Hell, earth, chaos, all; the argument
> Held me a while misdoubting his intent
> That he would ruin (for I saw him strong)
> The sacred truths to fable and old song
> (So Sampson groped the Temple's post in spite)
> The world o'erwhelming to revenge his sight.
> Yet as I read, soon growing less severe,
> I liked his project, the success did fear;

Marvell raises a problem. He concedes that the rendering of 'sacred truths' in 'fable and old song' (religious orthodoxy as literature) might create a separation, even a tension, between the Christian readers' sense of enjoyment and their code of belief. He believes that in this case it won't, but he does not say why. He praises Milton unreservedly, but he remains distant from any detailed engagement with the problem he raises.

To isolate a form of continuity between Marvell and Milton we might refer to the conclusion of the former's poem. He closes his celebration of Milton's achievement by referring not to the theology of *Paradise Lost* but to its style (45–54). Compare this with Milton's note on 'The Verse'. It might seem somewhat eccentric to us, in an era dominated by free verse and prosodic irregularity, to give so much prominence to the fact that this poem does not rhyme. Here we need a few contextual details.

Before the publication of *Paradise Lost*, unrhymed blank verse was regarded as occupying a kind of middle ground between poetry (certainly literary) and prose (not exclusively literary). Playwrights, Shakespeare in particular, could poeticize their dramatic texts by writing in blank verse, but in order to satisfy the abstract formal criterion for acceptance as non-dramatic poetry, verse had to rhyme. With *Paradise Lost* Milton effectively altered the history of English verse form.[1] He created a precedent that would later be invoked in Thomson's *The Seasons* and Wordsworth's *Tintern Abbey* and *The Prelude*. Thus we now begin to understand why Marvell felt it necessary to end his poem with a defence of this revolutionary gesture. In the note, Milton makes the daring claim that his poem has overturned and rejected an entire tradition of poetic writing and returned English poetry to the 'ancient liberty' of 'Homer in Greek, and of Virgil in Latin'.

A question should now have occurred to you. What has this emphasis on technique to do with the relation between literary writing and religious belief? Marvell's poem implies rather than states a connection, but let us consider a few possibilities. Milton was effectively breaking the rules of genre and expectation. He knew that he was cutting a very fine path between the extravagances of literary writing and the certainties of Christian belief, so perhaps his 'things unattempted' demanded a 'style unattempted'. Contemporary criticism shows that he succeeded in throwing the reader off balance in the sense that while acknowledging that no one before had attempted to rewrite scripture as literature, seventeenth- and eighteenth-century readers were also perplexed by the lack of a precedent in English for his peculiar method of poetic composition.[2] Perhaps his reinvention of poetic writing was an attempt to create a new medium, somewhere between the figurative adventures of poetry and the expository, factual discourse of religious prose. This would add another dimension of originality to line 16; the 'things unattempted' would be rendered in a form for which the reader could find no immediate point of comparison 'in prose or rhyme'. So much for the grounds of his revolutionary form. **What are its practical effects? Try to recreate the expectations of seventeenth-century readers. This is a nondramatic poem, but its style and prosodic structure do not correspond with poems they know. It might remind them of dramatic verse, but how are they supposed to reconcile the distinction between this genre and such non-dramatic epics as Spenser's *The Faerie Queene*, which maintain the conventional non-dramatic formulas of rhyme and the stanza? Moreover, how will this innovative stylistic gesture affect their, no doubt uneasy, perception of a poem which follows the unchallenged story of their origins?**

DISCUSSION

Read the opening section again and compare your experience of the structure and movement of the verse with that created by a rhymed poem. The most obvious point to make is that unlike rhymed poetry, blank verse does not fit the structure of the words and the syntax into such a tight and pre-ordained form; we are not detained by the insistent presence of a regular pattern. But has Milton abandoned form altogether and gone for a kind of rhythmic prose? I would say not. His pentameters operate as axes between pattern and freedom. The lines don't end merely because he has come to the tenth syllable; they supplement the coherence of syntax by causing the reader to admire the copresence of poetic precision and craftmanship with the irregular movement of speech. In the first two lines 'the fruit' is, appropriately enough, left hanging at the pause of the line ending. This makes us think again. Is it the literal fruit which Adam and Eve will eventually eat, or the figurative fruit of their gesture which has 'brought death' into the post-lapsarian world? In effect, both.

Now read this section again and pay some attention to how the free-flowing movement of the verse form is checked and counterbalanced by the peculiarities of Milton's syntax. For instance the object of the opening sentence 'mans first disobedience' stays in the mind for five lines before we find its verb and subject, 'sing heavenly muse'. As we read further into the poem we will find that such rearrangements of normal syntactic structure effectively dominate the style of the text. Two questions should be considered: Why does he do this? More specifically, how will these stylistic idiosyncrasies affect our impressions not only of Milton but of the reported speech patterns of the other figures in the poem?

It has been argued (Prince 1954, and Emma 1964) that, although Milton wrote in English, his use of latinate constructions would remind his classically educated readers of the epic pre-Christian tradition with which he sought comparison. At the same time such readers would also be reminded of the English dramatic tradition in which the characters of a narrative – a Shakespeare play for instance – spoke in blank verse. I would argue that he sought to engage with and transcend both traditions. When we come to the speeches of Satan, God, Adam and Eve, we will on the one hand encounter the freedom of unrhymed poetry – Dryden called blank verse *prose mesurée*, measured prose – but we will also find that he maintains the uniquely Miltonic style and idiom of his first person introduction. So we will listen to Satan, God, Adam and Eve, but we will be aware that their presences are effectively controlled and created by the author of the text. This is an important point because it relates to Milton's acknowledgement that he is creating fictional, literary counterparts for figures who constitute the basis for the Christian reader's code of belief and existence. Perhaps his style is designed to remind the reader that our encounters with biblical and supernatural figures can only take place through the shared medium of language. His style is his signature; we are not listening to the real voices of Satan or God, but to impressions mediated by the stylistic and imaginative skills of John Milton.

Let us consider the points raised so far. Milton is engaged in a literary enterprise for which there is no precedent in English. He will tell the story of the beginning of the human race and in doing so will provide the reader with a new and, it is implied, enlightening perspective upon the Old Testament narrative. As a literary text *Paradise Lost* will equal the epic grandeur of Virgil and Homer, but it will reach beyond the classical frame of reference and engage with the fundamental and absolute issue of human existence, man's relationship with God. With these perplexing objectives in mind, read the rest of Book I.

Book I is divided into three sections: the opening, which we've already considered; lines 27–83 in which Milton introduces the reader to Satan and his 'horrid crew'; and the substance of the book from line 84 onwards in which Milton shares his third person description with the voices of Satan and Beelzebub.

The issue that has drawn the most critical attention is Milton's portrayal of Satan, or, to be more accurate, Milton's creation of a series of speeches through which Satan portrays himself. **Read what have been regarded as his most powerful and emotive speeches (84–124 and 241–264). What impression do you get of Satan? Do these speeches modify our traditional notion of Satan as the embodiment of evil, yet at the same time detached from the contingencies and questionings of human experience? Crucially, do you feel any sense of sympathy with his predicament?**

DISCUSSION

Milton seems to me to be deliberately causing a conflict, a tension in the readers' response to Satan, between our perception of the character in the text and our notion of a personified idea that, irrespective of our personal code of belief, is part of our language and consciousness. In the first speech, which is clearly designed to raise the spirits of Beelzebub, his second in command, Satan displays a degree of heroic stoicism in defeat: 'What though the field be lost?/All is not lost' (105–6). These military images have prompted one major critic of the poem, William Empson, to compare him with a defeated general, reviewing his options and refusing to disclose any sense of final submission or despair to his troops. By the time we get to the second speech this sense of stubborn tenacity has transformed itself into composure and authority.

The mind is its own place, and in itself
Can make a heaven of hell, a hell of heaven.
What matter where, if I be still the same,
And what I should be, all but less than he
Whom thunder hath made greater? Here at least
We shall be free; the almighty hath not built
Here for his envy, will not drive us hence:
Here we may reign secure, and in my choice
To reign is worth ambition though in hell:
Better to reign in hell, than serve in heaven.

(254–64)

Where else might we find a speech to stand comparison with Satan's blend of confidence and rhetorical power? The most obvious intertextual correspondences will be found in Shakespeare. Henry V addressing his troops, Mark Antony stirring the passions of the crowd or even Richard III giving expression to his personal conception of the political future, all exert the same command of the relation between language, thought and effect.

It is intriguing to consider the difference in structure between the first and second speeches. The former is inspired, yet speculative; it consists of a series of questions and possibilities. The latter is precise, relentless, certain: 'The mind *is* its own place' ... 'We *shall* be free' ... 'We *may* reign secure', and that final line whose arrogant symmetry has turned it into an idiom, a cliché, of common usage 'Better to reign in hell, than serve in heaven'.

It is at this point that we should take a step back and ask ourselves a question that has troubled commentators on the poem since its publication. Ought we to feel comfortable in our appreciation of Satan's heroic stature? Despite the textual similarities between Satan and his Shakespearean (and classical) counterparts, the fact remains that in Christian belief, or in the modern context of popular mythology, he is the devil, the personification of all that decent humanity should reject and despise. Don't we then have to ask why Milton has chosen to create a pattern of sympathy, even admiration, between the reader and this source of evil? To address these problems, if not to resolve them, let's examine the way that Milton inserts himself into the texture of the speeches and exchanges between the devils, which left alone would dominate the book. An analogy might be posed. What would happen if Shakespeare had created a role for himself as creator and controller of his plays? He could stop the performance and introduce a second, commanding opinion on what the characters are and what, through their own speeches, they disclose to the audience. This, in effect, is what Milton does. Consider this third person interjection between Satan's first speech and Beelzebub's reply.

> So spake the apostate angel, though in pain,
> Vaunting aloud, but racked with deep despair.
> (125–6)

Milton is not telling anyone familiar with the biblical account of the fallen angels anything that they would not already know, but perhaps he finds it necessary to draw such a reader back to this condition of awareness, and away from an admiration for the very human attributes of tenacity, one might say heroism, against impossible circumstances. The subtext is that 'Satan might not sound like a figure racked with pain and in deep despair but I must remind you that he is'.

Use the relation between Satan's opening speeches and Milton's interjection as a point of comparison for the much broader series of correspondences between the spoken discourses of the fallen angels and Milton's function as a commentator. Consider Milton's detailed and lengthy description of the fallen angels (392–587). Some critics of his style, F.R. Leavis in particular, have cited such passages as examples of a tendency towards grandiose monotony (see Chapter 5, pp. 82–3). Milton is certainly precise, almost obsessive, in his enumeration of physical and behavioural horrors that attend the Satanic crew, but rather than detain ourselves with judgements of stylistic quality, let us consider the question of why he felt it necessary to draw the reader through this itemized account of the devils. The catalogue opens with Moloch.

> First Moloch, horrid king besmeared with blood
> Of human sacrifice, and parents tears.
> (392–3)

No one would quarrel with the scriptual accuracy of this description, but Milton has been rather imaginative with chronology. At this point in the history of the cosmos, children, parents and the blood of sacrifice did not exist. Indeed his whole account of the sordid tastes and activities of the devils is updated to give emphasis to their effects upon humanity. Again we have cause to suspect that Milton is attempting to match the reader's impulse to sympathize with the heroic, in Satan's case almost charismatic, condition of the devils with a more orthodox perception of them as a threat to the spiritual ideals of humanity. Later (777–92) he employs the mock heroic style and presents the devils as pygmies, shrunk to a physical status that mirrors their spiritual decadence. It could be argued that he wishes to forestall the reader's admiration of the effort and skill in the building of Pandemonium (710–92) by ridiculing its builders. The principal figures of Homer's and Virgil's poems are our original heroes – indeed the

terms heroic and epic poetry are interchangeable. The classical
hero will face apparently insurmountable tasks and challenges and
his struggles will effectively determine the narrative of the text.
Milton's conclusion of Book I with a mock heroic passage should
remind us of the problems he faces. Satan might well recall the
heroism of Ulysses, but he inhabits another sphere of belief. Our
instincts might prompt sympathy but the Christian code will
remind us that Satan struggles not against the shifting circumstances of fate and the fickle demands of the gods but against the
overarching presence of a single God, a single source of love, truth
and certainty. At least it will if we are Christians. If not, the text
offers even more interpretive difficulties.

Summary

The most striking and perplexing element of Book I is the fissure
opened between Milton's presence as the guide and co-ordinator
in the narrative and our perception of his characters as self-
determined figures. This splitting of the reader's attention will
become more complex and problematic as we proceed through the
poem, and we should, at this point, attempt to stabilize our
responses and consider the interpretive problems raised. Would it
be tenable to claim that Milton is engaged in a struggle with
his own powers of rhetoric and creativity? Since the eighteenth
century, critics and creative writers have sensed a degree of unease
between Milton's presentation of Satan as a tragically heroic
figure and his duty to remain faithful to the orthodox Christian
polarity of Satan (Evil) and God (Good). Blake (followed by
Shelley) claimed that Milton was of the 'Devil's party' without
being able to acknowledge this allegiance (see Chapter 5, pp. 80–
81). In this century A.J.A. Waldock (1947) and William Empson
(1961) have subjected the text to what might be termed a humanist
reading, detaching it from its doctrinal origins and judging the
characters in relation to their fictive identities, rather like the
characters of a novel. In their readings Satan emerges as a figure
whose responses to defeat and failure engage the reader in the
most intuitively human sense of identification.

    None of these interpretations resolves the fundamental
problem of why a writer of Milton's unquestioned skill could
disclose affiliations and sympathies that he was unable to control.
It is clear from his meticulous third person descriptions of the
Satanic crew that he was aware of the effect that their dramatic
presence would have on the reader. If he knew that Satan's skill
with oratory and his impressive sense of authority might prove

attractive to the reader, why did he not subdue them? The possibility that I urge you to consider, but not necessarily accept, is that he consciously and deliberately instituted a pattern of identification and sympathy between Satan and the reader. His reason for pursuing such a dangerous and paradoxical course will, I hope, become apparent.

Book II

Book II is divided into two sections. The first (1–628) consists of a debate, in which members of the Satanic Host – principally Satan, Moloch, Belial, Mammon and Beelzebub – discuss the alternatives available to them. The second is effectively the beginning of the narrative of the Fall: the devils have come to a decision and Satan sets out, via encounters with Sin, Death and Chaos, for Earth (629–1055).

Once again we face the problem of why and how Milton is manipulating the reader's foreknowledge of the narrative. Any contemporary reader of *Paradise Lost* would know, from Genesis, that Satan takes it upon himself to corrupt God's new creation, Man. So why does Milton detain such a reader for more than half a book with the debate which results in this decision? To engage with this question it would be useful at this point to contextualize the poem in relation to Milton's own experience of seventeenth-century society, history and politics.

Read the four major speeches of the debate: by Moloch (50–105), who argues for a continuation of the war with God; by Belial (118–228) and Mammon (237–83), who encourage a form of stoical resignation; and by Beelzebub (309–416) who raises the possibility of an assault upon Earth. The fact that these arguments are presented within an apparently rational, one might almost say democratic, forum of exchange is as significant as what they actually say. The most obvious point of comparison, for the seventeenth- *and* the twentieth-century reader, is Parliament, but the possibilities of reading this section as an allegory are fraught with potential problems and contradictions. Nevertheless, the relationship is worth examining.

DISCUSSION

Milton started writing *Paradise Lost* around the time of the collapse of the post-civil war Cromwellian Protectorate – a period in which England had been governed by Parliament and committee and in which Milton had functioned as a powerful civil servant and pro-Cromwellian propagandist. Is it possible that the devil's debate could relate in some way to Milton's perceptions of the post-civil war Parliament, or to his more immediate experience of the governing council, whose meetings he attended and served as Secretary of Foreign Tongues? Let us consider some facts and possibilities.

Milton was a Cromwellian. He welcomed Cromwell as God's chosen instrument for the preservation of true protestantism and its secular counterpart in a just social and political structure. But his allegiances and his political duties were attended by the uneasy consequences of a single event, the execution of Charles I. Milton's prose pamphlets *Eikonoklastes* and *Pro Populo Anglicano Defensio* (*In Defence of the English People*) were effectively attempts to justify regicide and republicanism against the growing mood of guilt and distaste at a regime which had based its right to govern upon an act which had overturned a millenium of Christian and political belief. With this in mind compare the following extracts. The first is from Milton's *Eikonoklastes*, his defence of regicide, and the second is from the opening of Moloch's speech to the Satanic Host.

> (remember) those faithful and courageous barons, who lost their lives in the field, making glorious war against tyrants for the common liberty ... But now with a besotted and degenerate baseness of spirit, except some few, who yet retain in them the old English fortitude and love of freedom, and has testified it by their matchless deeds, the rest enbastardised from the ancient nobleness of their ancestors, are ready to fall flat and give adoration to the image and memory of this man, [i.e. Charles I] who hath offered at more cunning fetches to undermine our liberties, and put tyranny into an art, than any British king before him.   (Yale, III, pp. 343–4)

My sentence is for open war: of wiles,
More unexpert, I boast not: then let those
Contrive who need, or when they need, not now.
For while they sit contriving, shall the rest,
Millions that stand in arms, and longing wait
The signal to ascend, sit lingering here
Heaven's fugitives, and for their dwelling place
Accept this dark opprobrious den of shame,
The prison of his tyranny who reigns
By our delay? No, let us rather choose
Armed with hell flames and fury all at once
O'er heavens high towers to force resistless way,
Turning our tortures into horrid arms
Against the torturer; when to meet the noise
Of his almighty engine he shall hear
Infernal thunder, and for lightening see

> Black fire and horror shot with equal rage
> Among his angels.
>
> (51–68)

There are some curious correspondences here. The angelic host at the time of Satan's uprising found themselves, like the English nobility, split between allegiance to and revolt against a 'tyrannical' ruler. After the civil war the Cromwellians, like the fallen angels after the Satanic rebellion, have established for themselves a republic and are now enjoying a degree of self determination – Milton's evocation of 'English fortitude and love of freedom' recalls Satan's earlier claim that 'Here at least/we shall be free' (I, 258–9). But it would be absurd to argue that Book II is offered by Milton as a direct allegory on the post-civil war experiment with republican government. To do so we would have to assume that Milton had renounced his Cromwellian allegiances and come to regard the execution of the king as comparable with a revolt against God, which he did not. To understand why Milton echoed his own republican arguments in his representation of the devils we should consider the events that had taken place between the writing of these two pieces.

With the death of Cromwell in 1658 the fabric of the republican government began to crumble. The army forced the resignation of his son, Richard, who had been appointed to succeed him as Protector and, within eighteen months, Charles II rode into London amid scenes of extravagant rejoicing. But the Restoration of the Monarchy in 1660 did not involve a return to the pre-civil war system of government. Parliament, or to be more accurate, the factions and interests that controlled Parliament, still represented the centre of political power. The principal change was in the removal from the centre of the individuals and the beliefs that had sustained the uncertain and very often chaotic form of open government of the Protectorate. In effect there were two types of Cromwellian: those who believed in and sought to maintain a new and unprecedented form of government through which the different classes and interests of the nation would be represented in Parliament, and those who had for whatever reason found themselves on the winning side in the civil war and who believed that after the death of the Lord Protector their own, or, to be charitable, the nation's interests would be best served by a form of compromise, the beginnings of what we now understand to be constitutional monarchy. Milton belonged to the former group, and indeed his last minute, pro-republican pamphlet *The Ready and Easy Way to Establish a Free Commonwealth* was published within a few weeks of the Restoration. The most divisive and bloody issue of the early Restoration was the memory of the execution of Charles I, and those who had urged against the execution united with the returned Royalists to take revenge upon the more conspicuous regicides. Milton, as the most famous Cromwellian propagandist, escaped imprisonment and possible execution partly through the intervention of his friend Andrew Marvell MP, and partly because his recent blindness was accepted by his accusers as a form of God-sent punishment. Consider Milton's perceptions of these political and personal reversals, perceptions which would be present during his writing of *Paradise Lost*. The new form of social and political organization for which the civil war had been fought was no longer even a possibility. Milton had contributed many tracts to the debate on what this new society should be and do. *Of Education* argued for modern and imaginative methods of school and university teaching, *The Doctrine and Discipline of Divorce* promoted legislation which would allow the marital laws to operate beyond the boundaries of class and wealth, and the most famous of all his pamphlets, *The Areopagitica* appealed for freedom of the press. Then, through the 1660s, he had to face the certainty that none of the ideals and beliefs, which for so long had drawn upon his energies and talents as a thinker and writer, would never be realized.

We should hesitate before arguing that Milton actually sympathized with the condition of Satan and the fallen angels, but the tragic and darkly ironic correspondences between their circumstances and his cannot be ignored. The devils and the true Cromwellians had not been annihilated, but their original objectives and ambitions had become shrunken parodies.

DISCUSSION

Finding direct correspondences between the figures and events of *Paradise Lost* and those of seventeenth-century British history is, as you are now beginning to find, like stepping through a critical minefield. Two points should be considered. Have we, as modern readers, become so inured to the activity of seeking out psychological or political complexities in literary texts that we over-read *Paradise Lost*? Perhaps Milton did not intend the poem to be read outside of its biblical context? I think an examination of the most obvious circumstantial evidence would urge us to discount this. Milton and his contemporaries had experienced, within two decades, events which can only be regarded as apocalyptic; every system of philosophic, political and religious belief had been challenged and shaken. It is impossible to imagine that such an experience would not have some effect upon the writing of a poem which investigates the origins of the human condition.

Moving on to the second point, how do we balance what we know about Milton and his life with our response to his poem? Keeping in mind the problems raised so far, let us test our interpretive faculties against a question that has troubled modern historical interpreters. Who, if anyone, in seventeenth-century history is Satan supposed to represent? Some critics (notably Whiting 1964 and Bennett 1977) have regarded Satan and the devils as evocations of Charles I and the Cavaliers. Their argument is that Satan is a usurper whose resentment of the Son's elevation through the heavenly hierarchy parallels Charles's conception of himself as a kind of mortal deity. And we might recall the presentation in Book I of the devils as pretentious hedonists, 'sons/Of Belial, flown with insolence and wine' (I, 501–2), and compare this with the puritan view of the Cavaliers as decadent sensualists. Rather more interpreters have found correspondences between Satan and Cromwell. Cromwell is the failed revolutionary, whose attempt to replace kingship with republicanism turned out to be an unrealizable objective, just as Satan's own ambitions will be eternally constrained by the omnipotence of God (Fallon 1984 and Revard 1980). The best way of considering these interpretive problems is to stay as close as possible to Milton's own writings. Let us repeat the earlier exercise and compare a section from Book II with an extract from Milton's political tracts. The first quotation is from Beelzebub's speech, in which, having proposed an assault upon Earth, he considers who would best serve their interests in this enterprise – he refers, without naming him, to Satan. The second is from *A Second Defence of the English People* (1654) in which Milton fulfils his duties as apologist for the Cromwellian Commonwealth.

> But first whom shall we send
> In search of this new world, whom shall we find
> Sufficient? Who shall tempt with wandering feet
> The dark unbottomed infinite abyss
> And through the palpable obscure find out
> His uncouth way, or spread his airy flight
> Upborne with indefatigable wings
> Over the vast abrupt, ere he arrive
> The happy isle; what strength, what art can then
> Suffice, or what evasion bear him safe
> Through the strict sentries and stations thick
> Of angels watching round? Here he had need
> All circumspection, and we now no less

Choice in our suffrage; for on whom we send
The weight of all and our last hope relies.
(402–16)

Cromwell, we are deserted! You alone remain. On you has fallen the
whole burden of our affairs. On you alone they depend. In unison
we acknowledge your unexcelled virtue... All know you to be that
man Cromwell! Such have been your achievements as the greatest
and most illustrious citizen, the director of public counsels, the
commander of the bravest armies, the father of your country...
Your deeds surpass all degrees, not only of admiration, but surely of
titles too, and like the tops of pyramids bury themselves in the sky,
towering above the popular favour of titles. But since it is, not
indeed worthy, but expedient for even the greatest capacities to be
bounded and confined by some sort of human dignity, which is
considered an honour, you assumed a certain title very like that of
father of your country.   (Yale, IV, pp. 671–2)

The circumstantial and indeed the rhetorical similarities seem clear
enough. Milton, who once defended the status of Cromwell as
Lord Protector from threats at home and abroad, deploys the
same emotive energies in his representation of Beelzebub, faithful
second in command and apologist for Satan, who faces a similar
task of upholding the power and dignity of the angel's rebellion.
Even Milton's subtle argument that Cromwell deserves a better
status than that conferred by hereditary title echoes the devil's
desire to find a new hierarchy to replace the heavenly order. But it
is not as simple as that. Satan, as the reader is aware, is about to
set out upon a mission which will result in the wretched, fallen
condition of all humanity, a condition which could hardly be
more deeply felt than by Milton in the 1660s. Moreover, the
legacy of Eve's response to Satan's urgings will be inhabited by
all human beings, irrespective of their temporal ambitions and
endeavours. Could it be that Milton is leading the reader into a
cunningly laid trap? Consider the structure of Book II. The first
half will engage the reader – particularly the seventeenth-century
reader – in a process of recognition and immediacy; the devils
conduct themselves in a way in which is remarkably similar to the
political state of England in the 1650s. The second half shifts the
reader into a very different temporal and metaphysical state of
awareness. Satan is no longer human. At the Gate of Hell he meets
Sin, born out of his head when the rebellion was planned, and
Death, the offspring of their bizarre and inhuman coition (666–
967). Then he encounters Chaos, a presence and a condition
conducive to his ultimate goal (968–1009). The effect on the
reader of this split perspective is, perhaps intentionally, disorientating. First we respond to him and his fellows as disturbingly

human, then we are plunged rapidly into a very different state of response and understanding. He is now the superhuman origin or ally of all the most disagreeable conditions of humanity, Sin, Death and Chaos.

Now read Book II with these points in mind. How far do you find that its two halves leave you in a state of uncertainty. Can they be resolved? Or at least explained?

DISCUSSION

One way of explaining the conflict of responses to Book II is as follows. Milton is fully aware of the effect that the correspondences between Satan, Charles I and Cromwell will have upon the reader. He intends that our responses and our state of awareness of what the text is offering will be hard to reconcile. If Satan is Cromwell does it mean that an analogy is proposed between the regicides and the demonic rebellion? If Satan is Charles are we supposed to reverse this biblical/historical allegory? The problem that we are obliged to confront again and again is of how to locate abstract conditions of good and evil in tangible human presences and beliefs. The punch line is delivered in the second half of the book. Satan is equated with the final and ultimate condition of evil and distress, but we are still unable to establish any certain parallel between this cosmological abstract and its real and immediate counterpart in specific human beings and beliefs. If any correspondence can be drawn between the poem and Milton's experience of seventeenth-century history it is that we (Cromwellians or Royalists) have overreached ourselves in our assumption that we can determine our true relation to such absolutes as good and evil. You will find that the question raised by Book II is one which Milton will maintain throughout the poem: how can we negotiate a path between a world populated by figures whose language, emotions, ambitions and reflexes are apparently human and our nagging state of awareness that they are metaphors for events and conditions which are, literally, beyond our understanding? Why should this be so? Because one result of the Fall was that human beings must exist at a much greater distance from God than did Adam and Eve in their pre-lapsarian state. Our sense of reason, justice, motivation, free will are partial and severely limited by the legacy of our original sin. So Milton, by presenting an image of the cosmos before the Fall, is offering us both a lens and a mirror. We see ourselves in the characters of Satan, Beelzebub and, in due course, God, Adam and

Eve, only because our range of awareness and understanding is enclosed and conditioned by our status as fallen beings.

As we shall see, critics have developed a variety of approaches to this conundrum, approaches which we will respond to in terms of our personal beliefs and religious affiliations. These can range from C.S. Lewis's reading of the poem as a kind of instructive guide to the power of Christian faith, to Waldock's and Empson's humanist readings in which Satan emerges as a more engaging character than God. With regard to the relation between Satan and seventeenth-century history, Christopher Hill, the Marxist historian, is the most radical of the humanist critics. In *Milton and the English Revolution* (1977) he argues that Milton uses the Satanic rebellion as a means of displacing his own 'deeply divided personality'.

According to Hill, he finds a form of consolation in creating Satan as a mirror image of the human paradox of ambition and failure.

> Satan, the battleground for Milton's quarrel with himself, saw God as arbitrary power and nothing else. Against this he revolted: the Christian, Milton knew, must accept it. Yet how could a free and rational individual accept what God had done to his servants in England? On this reading, Milton expressed through Satan (of whom he disapproved) the dissatisfaction which he felt with the Father (whom intellectually he accepted).   (pp. 366–7)

I shall not try to impose one or the other of these interpretations upon the reader, but before moving even further into the complexities of the poem we might try to think of any other literary text which confronts the reader with so uneasy a relation between personal perceptions and beliefs and the experience of reading. Kafka perhaps, or D.H. Lawrence or Shakespeare? The list could continue, but if critical history is an index to textual characteristics, then we must prepare ourselves for a text whose 'meanings' will be determined as much by the condition of the reader as by the intention of the author.

Books III and IV   God, Adam and Eve

Books III and IV engage the reader with two major issues of interpretation. How should we respond to a literary representation of God and what attitude should we adopt to our ancestors, and perpetrators of our fallen condition, Adam and Eve? The presence of the former dominates Book III and the latter Book IV, and their appearances are interspersed with accounts of the journey of Satan towards Earth.

But before considering these sections read the first 55 lines of Book III, generally known as the 'Address to Light'. This is effectively a second opening, in which Milton casts off the balanced impersonality of his third person presence and speaks directly to the reader. What is his purpose here?

DISCUSSION

The mood of the poem is about to change from the dominance of the Satanic host and the 'darkness visible' of hell to the 'light' of God and heaven. But why does he strike such an intensely personal and lyrical note, drawing attention to the light of God and to his own mortal condition of blindness? The section is important because of its subjectivity. Milton seems to pause for a moment and move outside his role as creator and co-ordinator of the great Christian epic. Can we learn anything from this which might assist us in our objective of understanding what he was trying to do in *Paradise Lost*?

An obvious point of comparison is his famous 'blindness' sonnet (No. XVII) written in the early 1650s when he first became aware of the fact that he was losing his sight. But this poem, with its mood of stoical resignation, tells us little more than we already know from the 'Address'. Let us look instead at two of his earliest poems, *L'Allegro* and *Il Penseroso*, written when he was in his early twenties, long before the civil war, Cromwell, blindness and the Restoration. These poems are the poetic equivalent of a debating exercise (a synkriseis) in which two sides of an argument are matched and counterbalanced, with the object of creating a kind of rhetorical symmetry. *L'Allegro* argues for the enjoyment of light, daytime, the pleasures of spring, and *Il Penseroso* considers the alternative pleasures of darkness, melancholy and contemplation. Compare the following quotations: the first from *L'Allegro*, the second from *Il Penseroso* and the third from 'Address to Light'.

1   While the rock with lively din
     Scatters the rear of darkness thin,
     And to the stack or the barn door
     Stoutly struts his dames before;
     Oft listening how the hounds and horn
     Cheerly rouse the slumbering morn,
     From the side of some hoar hill,
     Through the high wood echoing shrill;
     Sometime walking, not unseen
     By hedgerow elms, on hillocks green.
                    (49–58)

2 Hide me from Day's garish eye,
   While the bee with honeyed thigh,
   That at her flowery work doth sing
   And the waters murmering
   With such consort as they keep,
   Entice the dewy-feathered sleep
   And let some strange mysterious dream
   Wave at his wings in airy stream
   Of lively portraiture displayed
   Softly on my eyelids laid.

                         (141–49)

   Dissolve me into ecstasies
   And bring all heaven before mine eyes.

                         (165–6)

3   Yet not the more
   Cease I to wander where the Muses haunt
   Clear spring, or shady grove, or sunny hill,
   Smit with the love of sacred song; but chief
   Thee Sion and the flowery brooks beneath
   That wash thy hallowed feet, and warbling flow,
   Nightly I visit;

                         (26–32)

   So much the rather thou celestial light
   Shine inward, and the mind through all her powers
   Irradiate, there plant eyes, all mist from thence
   Purge and disperse, that I may see and tell
   Of things invisible to mortal sight.

                         (51–5)

Given that they are separated by three decades of traumatic experience the interrelationships between quotes 1 and 2 and quote 3 are quite astounding. As critics have remarked, *L'Allegro* gives the impression that Milton is performing a duty, listing and documenting the pleasures of the day in an effective though rather perfunctory manner. And it seems to me, from these brief extracts, that the tone of *Il Penseroso* is far more intense and committed than the lively, though somewhat unstructured, catalogue of *L'Allegro*. When we turn to 'The Address' it is almost as though this implied preference for dark contemplation over temporal pleasure has finally been realized and made explicit. The young, sighted poet's invocation of a 'strange mysterious dream' that will transform his actual experience into an internalized vision, 'on my eyelids laid' and 'bring all heaven before mine eyes' is a speculative metaphoric conception of seeing beyond the seen. But it is also a precise anticipation of the older, blind poet's satisfaction in his 'nightly visit', in the 'light' that 'shines inward' to disclose 'things invisible to mortal sight'. It is almost as though he was tempermentally and intellectually prepared for the relation between sensory deprivation and spiritual awareness three decades before blindness confronted him with a literal experience of this condition. So why did he choose to interrupt the narrative of *Paradise Lost* with this very personal state of being?

The 'Address' is intended to prepare the reader for an encounter with God and His Son. This is a potentially dangerous deployment of narrative because, as we have seen, the two opening books have created a very uncertain relation between the reader's awareness of his/her own human condition and an urge to identify with a superhuman figure, in this case Satan. What effect will this have on our reading of God? Think again about what Milton actually means in 'The Address'. He dwells upon the condition of blindness, but he also uses this as a literal correlative for the more complex spiritual experience of moving beyond the pleasures and the confines of the material, empirical world to an inner contemplative realm. We should remember here that Fallen Man is trapped within a cognitive and intellectual condition which is partial and limited. Perhaps he is reminding the reader that his forthcoming encounter with God, a God who will use that most human medium, language, will involve a temptation to judge His words and actions by our standards, that 'things invisible to mortal sight' are also things inconceivable to the fallen mind. Let's see.

God

Milton's presentation of God has led to as much uncertainty and division among modern critics as his characterization of Satan. We will examine the question of why this issue seems more problematic for modern readers in due course, but first let us go straight to the passage which has prompted so many diverse and conflicting interpretations, God's address to His Son (56–134). **Read through this exchange and consider the following questions. The will of God had often been the subject of literary writing but never had God and the Son featured so prominently as speaking characters. Why did Milton confront his readers with such a phenonemon? Do you find that your attention is split between the effects and the meaning of the exchange, and irrespective of your personal beliefs, the curious experience of listening to God?**

DISCUSSION

Before going into any detail about what God actually says, compare the style of the speech with that of any of the other figures encountered so far, including Milton. Metaphor is generally regarded as the definitive characteristic of poetic discourse, but can you find one instance of figurative language in this sequence? Were it not for the fact that the speech maintains the structure and rhythmic pattern of blank verse it could easily be mistaken for flat, almost impersonal, prose. Critics (particularly Stein, Empson, Waldock and Fish) have pondered the question of why Milton makes God's speech so conspicuously purposive and unadventurous, but let us conduct our own investigation.

What is a metaphor? In general it is a linguistic device that ascribes to some thing or action, a property or condition that it would not, in its usual context, possess. In Book I Satan claims that 'the mind is its own place, and in itself/Can make a heaven of hell, a hell of heaven' (254–5). This is metaphoric language; the mental condition, which is generally regarded to be intangible and insubstantial, is subtly but persuasively merged with images which refer to physical acts and concrete, specific locations. The usual distinction between thinking and making becomes, in this instance, a form of metaphoric fusion. The question of what effect such devices will have upon their recipient has divided thinkers and writers since Plato. It could be argued that in creating an unexpected resemblance between two objects or conditions the speaker/writer is attempting to clarify something which in normal discourse will not be evident. Alternatively, it has been claimed that by disrupting the stable relation between language and reality, metaphor allows its user to persuade the addressee of the validity of something that he wants them to believe, something which might seem to be true but which is primarily the result of the speaker's skill as a poet or rhetorician.[3]

Why then is this form of linguistic usage carefully subdued in God's speech? Consider Arnold Stein's conclusion, 'Poetry is human and metaphorical, and the Father's speeches are intended to express divine Justice as if directly: to seem without seeming: to create the illusion of no illusion' (1953: p.128). This seems clear enough; the need to use metaphor to persuade ourselves or others of the truth of something is part of our human, indeed of our fallen, condition, and although we can never hope to understand the mind of God we should at least attempt to strip his utterances of the human failings of poetry and rhetoric.

There are, however, a number of problems with this thesis. In attempting to detach God from the conventions of human rhetoric and thus to render his discourse factual and immune from the uncertainties of figurative language, is Milton admitting, by implication, that we will not be very pleased by what He has to say? Moreover, simply by abandoning metaphor, is it possible to prevent the reader from interrogating God's thinking and motivation in the same way that we have with Satan or Beelzebub? Whatever we might feel about the style of His discourse, He is still a character in a literary text and no matter how much our personal beliefs might urge us to suspend a literary response to the characterization of God it is very difficult to prevent ourselves from comparing Him with the other inhabitants of the narrative. Consider these questions in relation to what God actually says.

DISCUSSION

In effect he tells us that he is fully aware of what will happen in Eden, that Adam and Eve will fall and, as the Father/Son dialogue continues, that Christ will be required to redeem man. It is here that any potential for tension between our perception of *Paradise Lost* as a literary text and our awareness of its doctrinal context becomes most evident. If God already knows what will happen to His recently created species, then why should we, as readers, have to endure the lengthy and often painful account of the Fall. Moreover, if, as is later stated by Raphael to Adam, God created Man as a kind of replacement for the rebel angels, as a being who will eventually earn promotion to a more spiritual status, then there is clearly something peculiar about a figure who is supposed to be omnipotent and omniscient but who seems unable or unwilling to prevent the degeneration and eventual punishment of His own offspring. The Christian reader's answer to such a humanist interpretation would be that we have indulged our urge to identify with God in the same way that we troubled ourselves with the question of who Satan is supposed to represent; that conceptions of a temporal narrative, with events following one another according to a causal or even a random circumstantial framework, are part of our own limited conceptual realm. When we challenge the behaviour of God all we are doing is responding to our own corrupt and partial conceptions of reality. This may be a theologically valid point, but it could not prevent one of the most perceptive modern literary critics from responding to God as follows, 'But a parent who "foresaw" that the children would fall

and then insisted upon exposing them to the temptation in view
would be considered neurotic, if nothing worse; and this is
what we must ascribe to Milton's God' (Empson 1961: p.116).
Compare Empson with Lewis (1942).

> But it is heresy to say that God is corporeal. If, therefore, we insist
> on defining (which to the best of my belief, no Christian has ever
> been obliged to do) the mode of God's omnipresence we must not so
> define it as to make God present in space in the way in which a body
> is present.   (pp. 87–8)

Empson feels it necessary to compare God's behaviour with that
of a human parent, but Lewis feels that it is illogical – indeed
heretical – to perceive God as any kind of corporeal entity. The
tension between Christian and humanist readings deepens and
intensifies as the narrative proceeds, but for the moment let us
look again at God's speech to see if we can understand how it can
produce such a distressed, almost angry, response from an otherwise balanced and tolerant critic such as Empson. We know that
the speech maintains a precise, legalistic tone, but is there anything which allows (or tempts) us to imagine a real presence
behind the clinical discourse?

**Read the following passage and consider these questions. Given
that this is a first person address, making ample use of the pro-
nouns I, he and me, is it possible to suspend an imaginative and
judgemental construction of a fallible (human) speaker? If not,
what is Milton's intention in pitching the reader between recognition and an uncomfortable knowledge of who it is that we
recognise?**

So will fall

He and his faithless Progeny: whose fault?
Whose but his own? Ingrate, he had of me
All he could have; I made him just and right,
Sufficient to have stood, though free to fall.
Such I created all the etherial powers
And spirits, both them who stood and them who failed;
Freely they stood who stood, and fell who fell.
Not free, what proof could they have given sincere
Of true allegiance, constant faith or love,
Where only what they needs must do, appeared,
Not what they would? What praise could they receive?
What pleasure I from such obedience paid,
When will and reason (reason also is choice)

Useless and vain, of freedom both despoiled,
Made passive both, had served necessity,
Not me.

(95–111)

DISCUSSION

The whole sequence is rather oddly organized, in the sense that God seems to be positing and responding to a number of hypothetical questions and charges: 'Whose fault/Whose but his own'; 'I made him just and right'; 'What pleasure I'. Suspend for a moment your awareness of who is speaking and try to construct a character from the pattern of the language. Our closest point of comparison is a Shakespearian soliloquy, even Hamlet's, with its sequence of syntactic excursions and retreats. It cannot be denied that there is a very similar pattern of troubled uncertainty. Beneath each question and each answer there is the nagging insistent presence of a single issue; 'Have I treated Man badly?'

But, the Christian reader would now remind us that we are creating a psychological model that is, inevitably, a reflection of our own failings and anxieties. How do we resolve this conflict between Christian and humanist perceptions of God?

We might consult the critics. Stanley Fish (1967) has produced the most widely debated revision of the Empsonian approach, employing a method that has come to be known as New Historicism.[4] Fish, by comparing God's speech with a variety of seventeenth-century sermons and theological tracts, constructs a model of the contemporary reader. This person, he argues, would not be troubled by any political conflict between the literary presence of God and His biblical counterpart, because in the seventeenth-century mind 'God is God', an image, an idea, an eternal presence that will remain immune from the ambiguities and imponderables of human thought and language. This is Fish speaking for his putative seventeenth-century reader.

> To God belongs the essence of the speech, the completeness, the logical perfection, the perfect accuracy of its perceptions; all else is the reader's, the harshness, the sense of irritation, the querulousness. The monologue of the divine expositor . . . is dispassionate, and if we find it unsatisfactory the fault (quite literally) is ours. (p. 86)

This is an intriguing proposition, but it deepens rather than resolves our problem. The modern tension between Christian and humanist readings might well be a consequence of three centuries of enlightened scepticism, but each faction in the debate acknowledges, while disagreeing with, the position of the other, and

simply by reconstructing the allegedly seamless and unified responses of the seventeenth-century reader we cannot dispose of
our own sense of division. Without expecting to reconcile these
two positions, is there any way that we can accommodate both
within a broader, more pluralistic conception of the poem? If we
cannot, then we must carry through the text an awareness that,
depending upon our beliefs, we will be reading a different poem
from that experienced by someone else.

What, if anything, do modern Christian and humanist readers
have in common? Well, perhaps more than we might first think.
Christian readers such as C.S. Lewis believe that we are deceiving
ourselves if we expect to learn something new about God and
Providence from the writings of another human being, and that
we must regard *Paradise Lost* as a text which reminds us of two
states of human 'understanding'; that of which we know (patterns
of language temporal processes, cause and effect) and that of
which we cannot, as mortal presences, ever know (the true mind,
motivations and character of God). It is a poem about religion but
it should not be allowed to disturb the convictions and certainties
of religious faith.

> The cosmic story – the ultimate *plot* in which all other stories are
> episodes – is set before us. We are invited, for the time being, to look
> at it from the outside. And that is not, in itself, a religious experi-
> ence . . . In the religious life man faces God and God faces man. But
> in the epic it is feigned, for the moment, that we, as readers, can step
> aside and see the faces of God and man in profile.
>
> (Lewis 1942: 132)

Lewis claims that we must separate the literary from the religious
experience, while humanist readers such as Empson close this
intellectual and perceptual gap and claim that any conception
of God cannot remain immune from the perceived behavioural
patterns and limitations and the standards of reason, justice and
compassion engaged with by the God of Milton's poem. What
both agree upon, by implication, is that although we might not
share the same system of belief about God outside the text, we
cannot help but acknowledge that Milton's God engages in the
very human conditions of uncertainty, irritability and, it must
be stated, failure. So although we, as modern readers, might
experience a very different perception of the relation between the
text and the world, temporal or eternal, outside the text, we
should also accept that Milton in writing the poem has created his
own complex, self-contained universe which our own subjective
responses cannot change. We should not attempt to abandon
the tension between Christian and humanist readings, but our

appreciation of Milton the poet, rather than Milton the theologian or philosopher, might be more balanced and just if we concentrate on how he has created an artefact which can produce such a complexity of perceptions and responses. With this in mind let us proceed to an encounter with our ancestors.

Book IV   Adam and Eve

Book IV engages the reader in two narrative patterns that are both separate and interwoven. At times we are shown Adam and Eve conversing, praying and making love, and this vision of Edenic bliss is juxtaposed with wider perspectives on the arrival of Satan, his thoughts on Adam and Eve, and his encounter with the angels Gabriel and Uriel. This linguistic equivalent of the split-screen device is effective in the sense that it continually reminds us of the imminent challenge to the happiness and composure of the pre-lapsarian couple. Its effect upon our early perceptions of Adam and Eve is troubling, because we find ourselves unable to detach our perceptions of what they are from an insistent awareness of what they are soon to become.

Read the section from lines 288–538 and think about its structure. It consists of four voices: Satan, Adam, Eve and Milton, the co-ordinator and commentator. When reading literary texts, particularly novels in which a third person narrator describes and introduces a variety of characters, we will always find ourselves establishing an order of priority, based partly upon the intrinsic framework of the text and partly upon our own intellectual and tempermental disposition. One character will begin to stand out from the complex tissue of voices and descriptions either as someone with whom we sympathize or identify or as the dominant channel for our perceptions of what is happening in the text. Who dominates? And why? What is our relationship, as readers, with the different characters?

DISCUSSION

I find that there is a curious alliance between Satan and Milton. Not a moral or intellectual alliance, rather their shared condition as observers of events. Milton is clearly in charge, since he initially describes the arrival of Satan in the garden, but once Adam and Eve are introduced we find that we, like Satan and Milton, are watching them. The effect of this is peculiar, because as well as standing outside the text and, with the assistance of Milton,

watching Satan watching Adam and Eve we are also drawn into
it as Satan's fellow observers. One reason for this ordering of
impressions and positions might be that, as fallen readers, we are
much closer to the status of Satan than we are to Adam and Eve in
their pre-lapsarian condition. But enough of abstract speculation,
let's observe.

Adam's opening speech (411–39) and Eve's reply (440–91)
establish the roles and personal characteristics that will be main-
tained throughout the poem. Adam is the wise, though not
dominant, figure of authority who explains their status in Paradise
and the single rule of obedience and loyalty. Eve, in her account of
her first moments of existence, discloses a less certain, perhaps
impulsive, command of events and impressions. Her description of
her first moments of consciousness has received a great deal of
critical attention. Consider what we, and Satan, actually hear.

> That day I oft remember, when from sleep
> I first awaked, and found myself reposed
> Under a shade on flowers, much wondering where
> And what I was, whence thither brought, and how.
> Not distant far from thence a murmuring sound
> Of waters issued from a cave and spread
> Into a liquid plain, then stood unmoved
> Pure as the expanse of heaven; I thither went
> With unexperienced thought, and laid me down
> On the green bank, to look into the clear
> Smooth lake, that to me seemed another sky.
> As I bent down to look just opposite
> A shape within the watery gleam appeared
> Bending to look on me; I started back,
> It started back, but pleased I soon returned,
> Pleased it returned as soon with answering looks
> Of sympathy and love; there I had fixed
> Mine eyes till now, and pined with vain desire
> Had not a voice thus warned me, what thou seest,
> What there thou seest fair creature is thyself,
> With thee it come and goes: but follow me,
> And I will bring thee where no shadow stays
> Thy coming, and thy soft embraces, he
> Whose image thou art, him thou shall enjoy
> Inseperably thine, to him shalt bear
> Multitudes like thyself, and then be called
> Mother of human race: what could I do,
> But follow straight invisibly thus led?
> Till I espied thee.
>
>   (449–77)

The passage raises a number of interpretive problems, none of
which can remain immune from the uneasy presence of the others.

The principal decision that we, as readers, have to make is of whether this tissue of uncertainties is the result of the text coming adrift from Milton's full control, or of whether it is part of a deliberate strategy to unsettle or disorientate the reader. **What are these problems? We know from Genesis that Eve will be the first to eat the forbidden fruit. Does the style and texture of this passage lead us to believe that Milton's Eve will, like God, become a more disturbingly real figure than her biblical counterpart? Does this account of her first moments give us some idea of her temperament, her psychological condition?**

DISCUSSION

We hardly need textual notes or critical commentaries to tell us that Eve's attraction to her own image in the water (460–5) is a straightforward, and indeed candid, disclosure of narcissism. The implications are clear enough; the characteristics which would lead Eve to eat the forbidden fruit first are firmly in place in her earliest moments of conscious existence. It could be argued that Milton incorporates this self-fulfilling prophecy to make the details of the Fall psychologically plausible. Eve is seen by the reader and by Satan to be the more vulnerable partner, and this leads us back to the overarching notion of the reader as limited and restricted by our fallen condition. Is Milton sowing the seeds of our recognition of narcissism – and eventually personal ambition – in Eve in order to remind us, yet again, that our attempts to imagine existence before the Fall will result only in a reflection of our own defects?

A related possibility is that Milton and his contemporary readers would take it for granted that Eve, by virtue of her biological and psychological differences from Adam, functions as our means of understanding why the Fall was inevitable; that the distinction between male and female is a factor that has remained undiminished by our expulsion from Paradise. This raises the question of the origins and the validity of the relation between sexual and intellectual differences, and it would be wise to defer a lengthy discussion of this until the following chapter. For the moment let us look again at Eve's speech to see if there are any indications of how Milton intends the reader to respond.

Her use of the past tense is both conditional and deliberate. She is aware of her faults and has learned from God's instruction and advice ('Had not a voice thus warned me', 467). But does this mean that they can now face the uncertainties of temptation as equals? Consider her reported response to God's call, 'What could

I do/But follow straight, invisibly thus led?' (475–6). The key
term here is 'invisibly'. She responds not to God or Adam, because
she doesn't know they exist, but to 'a voice'. She can say later,
with retrospective wisdom, that this voice 'warned' her, but we
are left with the impression, presumably contrived by Milton, that
Eve is a person who responds instinctively to events and reflects
on them afterwards, a curious alliance of innocence, vulnerability
and retrospective wisdom.

Turn now to the style and structure of the speech. A point to
remember about Milton's verse form was raised at the beginning
of this chapter; the metrical freedom of blank verse allows characters to establish individual stylistic and intonational patterns.
Eve's speech is by no means uncertain or formally undisciplined.
When she tells of how she looked, 'into the clear/Smooth lake'
(458–9), she is performing a very subtle stylistic balancing act
between a contemporary usage of 'clear' as a substantive reference
to clarity of vision at sea ('the clear') and the word's eventual
relocation as a more familiar adjective ('clear smooth lake').
Similarly with, 'no shadow stays/Thy coming' (470–1), the pause
after 'stays' creates a tantalizing state of hesitation – 'stays' in the
seventeenth century could mean either 'prevents' or 'awaits'. The
impression generated by these hesitations and resolutions of meaning is that she is tentatively feeling her way through the traps and
complexities of grammar, and confirms our sense of her as half-
way between instinct and comprehension. But in making such an
observation we face a paradox. She betrays this apparent condition of ingenuousness (particularly compared with Adam's sense
of authority) by means of a number of subtle stylistic refinements.
Milton is either asking us to suspend our appreciation of the
formal dimension of the speech and accept this as his own means
of conveying her condition, or he is asking us to consider her as a
rather cunning actress and rhetorician, someone who can create
and perform her own persona. If the latter is the case, then the
implications are disturbing. Milton's Eve is far more sophisticated
and self-possessed than the Bible would have us believe. At the
heart of this question is Milton's difficulty in balancing what he
wants to tell us about his characters with the sense in which, once
released from his third person control, they begin to assume a life,
a literary presence, of their own.

Summary

I said earlier that the readers' sense of uncertainty regarding the
presentation of Eve might be a consequence of the text coming

adrift from Milton's full control. What I mean by this is that he has to tell a story that is already well-known and he must consequently face the possibility that his technique of fabulation might distort the original; Milton's Genesis might leave the reader with traces of meaning, fugitive possibilities, that are not present in the Bible. What should he do? Attempt to bring the text into line with scriptual orthodoxy or allow his skills as a poet and rhetorician to produce a text which reflects his personal conceptions of the relation between God and Man? The problem for us is of how to test our impressions of the literary text against Milton's theological or philosophical views. We know about his life and his experiences and we might surmise that his faith in God and in the certainty of Christian doctrine had been shaken by these, but we can't ask him. What we can do is to compare the problems raised by *Paradise Lost* not with scripture itself but with Milton's non-literary writings on scripture. The following is from his discourse *On Christian Doctrine* (1658) and in this passage he discusses, or rather pronounces upon, the same issues that we find dramatized in the first four books. If man is predestined to fall is it his fault, and in any case how can we, as the recipients of this legacy of sin, hope to understand such a potential paradox? **Read the passage carefully, if necessary more than once. Does it offer an unambiguous answer to our questions?**

> Everyone agrees that man could have avoided falling. But if, because of God's decree, man could not help but fall (and the two contradictory opinions are sometimes voiced by the same people), then God's restoration of fallen man was a matter of justice not grace. For once it is granted that man fell, though not unwillingly, yet by necessity, it will always seem that necessity either prevailed upon his will by some secret influence, or else guided his will in some way. But if God foresaw that man would fall of his own accord, then there was no need for him to make a decree about the fall, but only about what would become of man who was going to fall. Since, then, God's supreme wisdom foreknew the first man's falling away, but did not decree it, it follows that, before the fall of man, predestination was not absolutely decreed either. Predestination, even after the fall, should always be considered and defined not so much the result of an actual decree but as arising from the immutable condition of a decree. (Yale, VI: 174)

DISCUSSION

If after reading this you feel rather more perplexed and uncertain about our understanding of God and the Fall than you did before, you are not alone. Read it aloud to yourself or others and see if

your experience corresponds with mine. It is like being led blind-
fold through a maze. You start with a feeling of relative certainty
about where you are and what surrounds you, and you end the
journey with a sense of having returned to this state, but you are
slightly troubled about where you've been in the meantime. Can
we wrest an argument or a straightforward message from this
passage? It would seem that predestination (a longrunning
theological crux of protestantism) is, just like every other com-
ponent of our conceptual universe, a result of the Fall. Thus,
although God knew that man would fall, He did not cause (pre-
determine) the act of disobedience. As such, this is fairly orthodox
theology, but in making his point Milton allows himself and his
readers to stray in to areas of paradox and doubt that seem to run
against the overarching sense of certainty. For instance he concedes that 'it will always seem that necessity either prevailed upon
his (man's) will by some secret influence, or else guided his will in
some way'. Milton admits here that man will never be able to
prevent himself ('it will always seem') from wondering what
actually caused Adam and Eve to eat the fruit. Was it fate, the
influence of Satan, Adam's or Eve's own temperamental defects?

The passage certainly does not resolve the uncertainties
encountered in the first four books, but it does present itself as
a curious mirror-image of the poem. Just as in the poem the
immutable doctrine of scripture sits uneasily with the disorientating complexities of literature, so our trust in theology will
always be compromised by our urge to ask troubling questions.
Considering these similarities it is possible to wonder if Milton
decided to dramatize Genesis in order to throw into the foreground the very human tendencies of scepticism and self-doubt
that exist only in the margins of conventional religious and
philosophic thought. If so, why? As a form of personal catharsis,
as an encoded manifesto for potential anti-Christianity, as a
means of revealing to readers the true depths of their uncertainties? All of these possibilities have been put forward by commentators on the poem, but as the following chapters will show,
the decision is finally yours.

3. The Fall:
Books V–IX

Books V–IX chart the progress of Adam and Eve towards the
Fall. So far we have allowed our encounters with the text to
follow its narrative sequence, but with the issues to be dealt with
in this chapter it is time for a change of perspective. We should
not dispense with our awareness of the chronology of the poem
but we should supplement this with a greater command of its
complex network of themes and parallels. Treat this sequence of
events more as if it were a vast painting, across which you can
discern correspondences, cross-currents and juxtapositions.

The first thing to do is to read these books at one or two
sittings, rather as you would a novel. Then draw up in note form
what for you are the most prominent and problematic themes and
events. You can then return to the localities of the text and take
with you a map or diagram of its thematic landscape. You might
choose to emphasize the relationship between Raphael, the
pedagogic angel, and Adam his dutiful pupil; their exchanges
effectively dominate the narrative of Books VI to VIII. Alternatively you might find the fact that Eve moves into the background during this period of instruction as significant; she initiates
the Fall, but she receives a second-hand, summarized version of
Raphael's advice. The point of this exercise is not to direct you to
a 'correct' interpretive agenda; more to have you experience the
lead up to the Fall in Book IX as something that involves our
subjective response to the characters as much as it does our
perception of a sequence of events and facts. Your choices and
priorities will of course involve extensions, mergers and intensi-
fications of the questions raised in Chapter 2. For example, are
our perceptions of Eve from Book IV consistent with her pattern

of behaviour in Book IX? After reading through a detailed
account of Adam and Eve before and during the Fall, how do we
feel about God's judgement in Book III of man as an 'ingrate', 'he
and his faithless progeny', the despoilers of 'freedom'?

The following summary is based on my own exercise in
reading and reflection, but do not regard this as a final, authori-
tative list of priorities. Compare it with your own, and, as the
chapter proceeds, the reasons for any degree of divergence or
conflict should become apparent.

Structure and Pattern

I am struck first of all by the amount of space given to an account
of Adam's exchanges with the angel, Raphael. This begins at line
361 of Book V and is the dominant feature of the poem until the
end of Book VIII. Why? In practical terms it would seem to
provide the best means available for Milton to make the reader
more fully aware of the character and circumstances of Adam –
less so in the case of Eve since she either listens in or, when absent,
has the exchanges explained to her. Looked at more closely the
exchange becomes an ingenious narrative device. Books V and VI
involve an account of the war in heaven, and Book VII continues
this cosmological history with a description of God's decision to
create another world and a new race of beings. Adam has to hear
about all this, and who else can tell him? Raphael's instruction is
then turned into something like a tutorial, and for much of Book
VIII Adam tests his own perceptions of God, the Garden, the rule of
obedience, against the benevolent wisdom of his teacher. It is ingenious in two senses. First, after spending four books in the company
of Adam and Raphael it allows the reader a greater understanding
of the former's character and intellectual abilities. Second, when
we reach Book IX the dramatic effect of the Fall is intensified;
what had, for around 3,500 lines, been an unlikely yet fully understood hypothesis, becomes suddenly imminent and inevitable.

The function of Eve in this narrative presents us with a
problem. She is talked about and she is made aware of Raphael's
advice, but for most of the central section of the poem she exists
in the margins, to be moved suddenly back to the centre in Book
IX when she instigates their act of disobedience.

Before making use of our broader perspective upon the
themes raised in this sequence, let us return to chronology and
consider the opening of Book V in which Raphael is introduced as
a link between the Garden and the Cosmos. **Compare the opening
of Milton's 'Argument' to Book V with lines 219–245. In the
former Milton informs us in an impersonal, discursive manner of**

God's decision to send down Raphael, while in the latter we fi
ourselves again in the company of God as a speaking presence.
Are there problems in reconciling our perceptions of the God of
belief and scripture with our instinct to question the statements
and decisions of Milton's literary character?

DISCUSSION

Already, we encounter what will by now be a familiar sense of
tension between the biblical and the literary narratives. Why, we
might ask, does God feel it necessary to 'render man inexcusable',
'Lest wilfully transgressing he pretend/Surprised, unadmonished,
unforewarned' (244—5)? We know that man has free will and the
ability to resist temptation, but we also know that God knows
what his choice will be, and it thus seems rather odd that God
should use the conditional term '*Lest* wilfully transgressing'. A
whole series of questions are generated by this. If Milton assumes
that we will suspend our enquiry regarding the contradictory sense
of God pretending not to be omniscient then how will we deal
with a number of related problems. Does Raphael know that his
mission will be in vain? If so will this change our attitude to this
'sociable spirit'? As our questions begin to multiply we might also
speculate on why Raphael is advised to carry such a limited
amount of useful information. We must assume that God is aware
of what disguises Satan is currently adopting, and that the dream
experienced by Eve was a Satanic hallucination (prefiguring the
details of the actual Fall). Why then is Raphael told only to warn
Adam of an 'enemy' 'plotting now/The fall of others', 'by deceit
and lies'? (239—243). Consider Milton's problem: the reader can
observe the cunning machinations and disguises of Satan and we
are also aware of the vulnerable status of Adam and Eve (look
back to the Dream, 27—94). Then we find that the angel sent to
assist them against Satan is told to grant them a very limited and
partial awareness of the likely manifestation of this threat. It is
rather like watching the victim of imminent murder in a film or
play; we can see the murderer approaching his victim from behind
and we can also see, with his back to us, another character whose
awareness of this act, and his continued silence, is disturbing.
How does the creator of such an effect expect us to respond? In
our search for an answer to this we will encounter a series of
equally perplexing questions. Let us move on to lines 308—576.
  These are a microcosm of the tensions and complexities of the
five central books. The passage establishes the terms and conditions in which Adam's exchange with Raphael will take place,
and for reasons that are not easy to explain, it anticipates specific

events and behavioural patterns. Follow this passage through and consider its most prominent correspondences with the broader framework of the narrative. **Bear the following questions in mind. Is Milton's presentation of Adam and Eve a concession to contemporary (and modern) codes of male and female behaviour, or is he attempting to prepare the psychological ground for the fact that Eve falls first? In his first encounter with Adam and Eve does Raphael seem genuinely capable of assisting them in the forthcoming struggle with the rule of obedience?**

DISCUSSION

Preparing the Meal (308–404)

Given that we are supposed to be aware of our distance and detachment from the pre-lapsarian condition of our ancestors, the preparations for their first dinner guest bear a startling resemblance to the domestic protocols of seventeenth, and very likely twentieth-century England. Milton's description of Eve in her 'dispatchful' preparation of the food reads as a Restoration prototype for Mrs Beaton or Elizabeth David. We sense her anxiety that things should be just right for her first experience as hostess.

> She turns, on hospitable thoughts intent
> What choice to choose for delicacy best,
> What order so contrived as not to mix
> Tastes, not well joined, inelegant, but bring
> Taste after taste upheld with kindliest change.
>   (332–6)

Milton's words, but note that the hesitant pauses at 'mix/Tastes' and 'bring/Taste after taste' enact a slightly bizarre reminder of the uncertain account of her first moments of existence. It is as though Milton is unable – or unwilling – to detach his characterization of Eve from the conventional psychological and social model of 'female' behaviour. Milton's presentation of the first woman as a prototype for her successors in Christian society is something we should keep in mind, particularly when we come to the question of who initiated the Fall. For the moment we should note that Eve and her culinary enterprises are shifted into the background as Adam and Raphael move from genial greeting to more 'serious' issues.

Food and Spirits (404–505)

I place inverted commas around serious because this section, in which Raphael extends his explanation of how angels too can eat into a more complex discourse on the physical/spiritual components of existence, is the closest that the poem takes us to the comic, although the comedy is unwitting. Having said this I face the attendant question of whether it is only the modern reader who, viewing from a point of scientific superiority, will find amusement in all this. Judge for yourself; the discourse delays the meal and Milton finds himself with a small opportunity to remind the reader that things then were not quite the same as things now, 'A while discourse they hold;/No fear lest dinner cool' (395–6). Why? Because fire was part of the punishment of the Fall and, before this, food did not need to be heated.[1] This puts us in our place, but as the explanation proceeds we begin to recognize a theory of mortal and spiritual existence that is a merger of the theological and scientific orthodoxies of the seventeenth century. Raphael maps out a chain of being with the gross materiality of earth and water at the bottom and the spirituality of angels at the top. God Himself seems able to transcend these conditions of quantification. Man is somewhere in the middle, part spirit, part substance, but rather more limited than the Angel's in his ability to shift between transubstantial states – man can have spiritual thoughts but he cannot be a spirit. The crucial section of Raphael's address comes at lines 493–499.

> Time may come when men
> With angels may participate, and find
> No inconvenient diet, nor too light fare;
> And from these corporal nutriments perhaps
> Your bodies may at last turn all to spirit,
> Improved by tract of time, and winged ascend
> Etherial.

Here the faintly farcical notion of what Empson referred to as 'eating ourselves to Angelhood' takes on a darker shade. Raphael does not give precise details of their possible promotion to spirituality but his description is sown with a number of potentially disturbing clues. He implies, without really explaining, that there is some mysterious causal relationship between such physical experiences as eating and the gradual transformation to an angelic, spiritual condition. This would strike a familiar chord for Eve, because in her dream the tempter tells her to 'Taste this, and be henceforth among the gods/Thyself a goddess, not to earth confined' (V, 77–78). Later in Book IX, just before she eats the fruit, Satan plays upon this same curious equation between eating and spirituality, 'And what are gods that man may not become/As they, participating godlike food?' (IX, 716–17). It could be argued that Raphael's enigmatic comparison between 'corporal nutriments' and their eventual ability to 'ascend/Etherial' creates a kind of subliminal framework of possibilities whose final and most obvious solution is that they will benefit from eating the fruit. Several problems are raised here, both for the reader and for the participants in the narrative. Who planned these correspondences? Satan could surely not have known that his dream-vision would match the hypotheses of Raphael, but God (and His messenger) are fully aware of the similarities. It is difficult to stop ourselves from reflecting on the apparent malevolence behind all this, because Milton has obviously taken the trouble to foreground and emphasize the darkly ironic parallels between Adam's and Eve's awareness of what they might become and the circumstances which cause them to be denied this reward. If Milton has deliberately created this suspicion of the true activities of God; why? We shall return to the problem of understanding the circumstances of the Fall (for us and them), but before moving to this broader perspective, consider the section that operates as the preface to Raphael's story of existence.

Free Will and Knowledge (520–576)

Compare the two passages that seem to function as the grounds for Adam's understanding of Raphael's instructions: the explanation of free will (520–535) and the discourse on the limitations of man's knowledge of God and the cosmos (563–576).

In the first passage Adam is told (and the advice will be repeated) that their future will depend not upon some prearranged 'destiny' but upon their own decisions and actions. In the second, Raphael concedes that his salutary tale of the war in heaven and the creation of Man must be translated into the linguistic and conceptual mode that, at least for the present, restricts man's understanding of life and events beyond the Garden, and we are reminded of this at the end of his account of the war in Book VI (893–6).

One cannot help noting the potential for conflict here. Man's future depends upon his gifts of free will, but his supplementary gift of reason and knowledge, which will assist him in his decisions, is limited and partial.

Summary

The relation between the way Adam and Eve think and what they do will become even more problematic, and our response to this problem can lead us along diverse and sometimes contradictory interpretive tracks. Our sense of watching the inevitable is intensified by the knowledge that a number of the ideas which eventually precipitate the act of disobedience are already part of their state of awareness. We begin to wonder if God's objective of rendering man inexcusable is a thinly disguised strategy of allowing man enough rope to hang himself. True, man has free will, but the sense of choice and possibility attendant upon this condition is available only to Adam and Eve. Everyone else – God, Raphael(?), Milton, the reader – knows what will happen. But perhaps our awareness of this is designed to remind us, yet again, of the confinements of our own instincts and powers of reason. In our attempt to look back before the Fall we find only a mirror.

The Dangers of Reason

The need continuously to balance the two patterns of meaning created by the poem is a concession to the historical fact that modern readers will be divided between those who perceive the text in the way that we assume it was understood in the seventeenth century – the Christian readers – and those who will regard it as a cultural phenomenon whose roots in Christian doctrine are just one dimension, and by no means the dominant one, of its complex network of meanings. The consequent balancing act might well satisfy conditions of pluralism and tolerance but it continually obliges us to check and counteract our initial responses. By conceding that a humanist reading might not have occurred to a contemporary reader we necessarily limit its full impact and ramifications. What I mean by this is that the interpretive paths followed by critics such as Waldock and Empson disclose textual complexities and moral paradoxes that might well be marginalized by the steadying presence of doctrine and belief.[2] I am not implying that Christian readers such as C.S. Lewis, or indeed the majority of pre-twentieth-century commentators, lack the skill or sensitivity of their humanist counterparts, but their sense of certainty and assurance does impose certain limitations on what the reader feels able to assume or surmise. What I propose for the following section is rather different from the seesaw pattern of argument and counter-argument that has so far governed our method of reading. Let us allow the instincts and techniques of the humanist reader the dominant role, not in order to discredit or disprove Christian readings, but to see what conclusions and impressions we are left with after detaching the poem from the contextual preconditions and limitations of 'what it is supposed to mean'. Outer-textual references to seventeenth-century theology and empiricism are often capable of resolving problems by treating the reader and the text very much as an umpire would deal with a dispute in tennis; he might not be entirely sure if the ball was in or out but he knows the rules and the rules state that he is the final arbiter in such an exchange. We cannot dispense with the referee, but, to wring this metaphor dry, let us assume the feelings and perceptions of the player in this game of textual interaction. We will refer outside the text to writings by Milton and others, but we will be more cautious about allowing such enquiries to smother or dispel our own doubts and impressions.

We will start, as the title of this section indicates, with the problem of reason. To appreciate what Milton means by God's gift of reason we must base our assumptions more upon implication and circumstantial evidence than upon direct statement. Reason is a problematic concept because it works both within and outside the poem. We have already experienced the difficulties involved in imposing a rational, logical framework upon figures such as God and Satan, who exist beyond our realm of understanding yet communicate with us in language. Within the poem Adam and Eve have to deal with a similar problem. Should they simply respond to Raphael's discourse as a list of unchallengeable regulations or should they regard it as a prompter to purposive, rational enquiry? Stanley Fish on this problem: 'If the light of reason coincides with the word of God, well and good; if not, reason must retire, and not fall into the presumption of denying or questioning what it cannot explain' (1967: 242). So in the discussion that follows we will face two patterns of uncertainty: our own, in our attempts to judge Adam and Eve's use of the gift of reason; and their's in their attempt to deal with an apparently arbitrary rule with mental equipment that will prompt them to challenge and interrogate its logic.

DISCUSSION

Raphael in his description of creation in Book VII uses the term to distinguish man from other creatures.

> a creature who not prone
> And brute as other creatures, but endued
> With sanctity of reason, might erect
> His stature, and upright with front serene
> Govern the rest, self knowing, and from thence
> Magnanimous to correspond with heaven,
> But grateful to acknowledge whence his good
> Descends.
>   (506–13)

This seems straightforward enough. Man is the rational being whose self knowledge allows him to appreciate his position as superior to other creatures but loyal and subservient to God. To determine the full extent of this state of 'self knowing' we might recall Raphael's caution regarding the difficulty in 'measuring things in heaven by things on earth' (VI, 894). This sense of man's distance from the final and absolute truths of the universe permeates the whole of Raphael's discourse.

Read Book VIII, lines 84–178, in which Raphael describes the structure of the cosmos. More specifically, consider the reason for the opening section in which Adam is warned that what he is about to hear is a grossly simplified version of the actual state of the planetary system, which,

> the great architect
> Did wisely to conceal, and not divulge,
> His secrets to be scanned by them who ought
> Rather admire; or if they list to try
> Conjecture, he his fabric of the heavens
> Hath left to their disputes, perhaps to move
> His laughter at their quaint opinions wide.
>
> (73–78)

It seems to me that Milton intends this passage to operate at two levels, one involving the reader's perception of its effect on Adam and one involving its effect on the reader. The second relates to the seventeenth-century debate on the validity of the Ptolemaic or the Copernican models of earth and the planets. These arguments were theological as well as scientific, since our knowledge of the relative positions and movements of the planets would inevitably influence our notions of the location of heaven and hell. The first recontextualizes this contemporary issue within the broader message that Adam should not attempt to overreach his human limitations, and try to speculate on such matters as where exactly God is:

> God to remove his ways from human sense,
> Placed heaven from earth so far, that earthly sight
> If it presume, might err in things too high,
> And no advantage gain.
>
> (119–23)

The problem, for the reader, is how to deal with the co-presence of these two levels of meaning. In one sense we are invited to identify with Adam, to see our own adventures into cosmological theory as subject to the same limitations as his sphere of awareness and perception. But this pattern of correspondences is disturbing because we know that Adam, despite the good advice of

Raphael, will indeed attempt to overreach himself. So, perhaps
rather than identify with Adam's condition we ought, for our own
safety, to attempt to distance ourselves from it. This leads us back
to the question of why Adam and Eve, being fully equipped with
the faculties of reason and advised of their current deployment,
chose to perform an act which, in any rational judgement, verges
upon the suicidal?

With this question in mind, look at the second part of Book
VIII, in which Adam, encouraged by Raphael, rehearses his
understanding of himself and his condition.

The section that has drawn the most critical attention is
Adam's account of his conversation with God that resulted in the
creation of Eve (lines 357–451). Read this and draw up a summary of what actually occurs during the exchange. Mine is as
follows: Adam laments his solitude. God says, well you're not
alone, you have the other creatures, the angels and me. Yes, says
Adam, but I want an equal partner. God replies: Consider my
state. I don't need a consort. Adam returns, most impressively,
with the argument that God is a perfect self-sufficiency, but man
must be complemented in order to multiply. Quite so, says God.
This was my intention all along. And he creates Eve.

Consider both the form and the substance of this exchange. It
reminded William Empson of an educational phenomenon known
as the Rule of Inverse Probability. This is where the student faces
an intelligence test and realizes that more important than satisfying some absolute criterion of correctness or truth, he must
above all satisfy the expectations of the person setting the test. So
it is not, 'What is the correct answer?', but rather, 'What answer
am I supposed to give?'. Adam seems at first to be contradicting
God, but by using the reason that God has given him he eventually presents the case that God himself has already prepared.

**Given that we accept such an interpretation of the passage, what
does it mean? Consider the technique of parallels that Milton
incorporates into the broader narrative of the poem. The first of
these occurs in Books II and III where we are invited to recognize
similarities between the debate of the fallen angels in which Satan
offers to re-establish the battle with God by disrupting the progress of his new creation, and the exchange between God and the
Son who 'volunteers' to redeem fallen man (II, 432–66 and III,
238–65). Can we find a similar counterpart for Adam's exchange
with God? The most likely would seem to be Eve's conversation
with Satan in Book IX (532–779). Read this and consider what the
two passages suggest to us about Adam's and Eve's use of reason.**

DISCUSSION

First of all we should attempt to pull together a few narrative threads. Eve when approached by Satan would seem to have attained the same level of intellectual acumen as Adam. She was absent for much of the discussion in Book VIII, but we know that she overheard parts of it (IX, 275) and, more importantly, that she had it explained to her by Adam (VIII, 50–1). She knows that God's method of instructing them is subject to unexpected visitations: they are not warned of Raphael's arrival, Adam's exchange with God is apparently unplanned, and she can remember being advised against narcissism by a mysterious 'voice' that later turns out to be God. So when she first encounters this curious beast endowed with the power of speech, she has no reason to assume that this is not another stage in the gradual process of enlightenment and disclosure. She is of course aware of some threat to their position, but she does not know what form this will take, so her response to this presence will depend entirely upon her rational judgement of its discourse.

Satan's speeches, particularly the second (678–733), involve an impressive and logical deployment of fact and hypothesis. Eve does not understand the meaning of death, the punishment to be visited upon them after eating the fruit, so Satan explains.

>   ye shall not die:
> How should ye? By the fruit? It gives you life
> To knowledge. By the threatener? Look on me,
> Me who have touched and tasted, yet both live,
> And life more perfect have attained than fate
> Meant me, by venturing higher than my lot.
> Shall that be shut to man, which to the beast
> Is open?
>   (685–93)

Having raised the possibility that death is but a form of transformation beyond the merely physical, he delivers a very cunning follow up.

> So ye shall die perhaps, by putting off
> Human, to put on gods, death to be wished,
> Though threatened, which no worse that this can bring.
> And what are gods that man may not become
> As they, participating godlike food?
>   (713–17)

Place yourself in Eve's circumstances and think back to Raphael's explanation of their eventual ascent to angelhood. Does this not sound very much like the missing explanation of how this will take place? He even hints at such a continuity with his reference to 'godlike food'.

Eve's speech, both to Satan and to herself, takes the form of a reasonably incisive commentary on his propositions. Satan asks, 'wherin lies/The offence [to God], that man should thus attain to know?' (725–6). Eve replies, 'In plain then, what forbids he but to know/Forbids us good, forbids us to be wise?' (758–9), and expands on the hypothesis, 'What fear I then, rather what know to fear/Under this ignorance of good and evil,/Of God or death, of law or penalty?' (773–5). A paraphrase of this last statement would be something like 'We have been advised of our ignorance, yet promised enlightenment. Perhaps the rule of obedience is part of God's existential puzzle. Our fear of the penalty might be all that prevents us from a fuller understanding of the ways of God?'.

The correspondences between this exchange and Adam's account of his conversation with God are striking and rather disturbing. They both take the form of what is known as a Socratic dialogue. Socrates, the teacher, will not impose a belief or a truth on his pupil, but will sow his discourse with enough speculations and possibilities to engage with the latter's faculties of enquiry and reason, and through this exchange of propositions and questions they will move together toward a final conclusion. Thus we are faced with the unedifying possibility that not only does God foresee the Fall, he even scrupulously provides his creatures with just the right sort of mental equipment to make the Fall inevitable. Even Milton, in his third person interjection between Satan and Eve concedes that 'his persuasive words, impregned/With reason, to her seeming, and with truth' (736–7). It is reason, the faculty that would enable them to cope with free will, that is the prominent factor in her decision. True, they are told time after time that the rule of disobedience is immutable, but since their first moments of existence they have been subjected to a continuous barrage of new disclosures, enlightenments, advice that things are not quite as they first thought they were. They are aware that their observance of the rule is a token of their love and loyalty, but as Satan implies, such an edict is open to interpretation.

> What can your knowledge hurt him, or this tree
> Impart against his will, if all be his?
> Or is it envy, and can envy dwell
> In heavenly breasts?
>
> (726–30)

We could continue with the case for our ancestors' defence.

Returning to Book VI, for instance, how is Adam supposed to fully comprehend the parallels between the Satanic revolt and the rule of obedience if he has not yet experienced the former's motivating force, envy? Moreover, the lengthy and elaborate description of the battle is brought up to date by Milton with the invention of machines resembling cannon. This might, for the contemporary reader, stir uneasy memories of the civil war, but what use is this to Adam whose education in the particulars of violence and death must wait until his post-lapsarian encounter with Michael? In any event no one dies in these battles, and if they were intended as reminders of the punitive resources of an all-powerful deity, then as Eve, and later Adam, demonstrate in their reflections on the consequences of the Fall, such an effect was negligible. All of this contributes to a suspicion that God and Raphael load their instruction with so many uncertainties, imponderables and logical conundrums that Adam's and Eve's eventual choice to investigate the meaning of the rule becomes an inevitable consequence of their state of awareness. Consider the chronology of events. God sees Satan in the Garden and sends Raphael to 'render man inexcusable' (see 'Argument' to Book V and lines 224–45). We don't know what would have happened had they been left without this advice, but there is certainly evidence from Eve's replies to Satan that the consequences of his educational policy are of considerable benefit in the devil's pursuit of his objectives.

These readings belong, as I've said, to the humanist school of interpretation, and it is time to consider my advice to defer an engagement with the Christian school. I will now clarify my reasons for directing the reader in this way and it will be up to you, in the following section and beyond, to judge the validity or wisdom of my thesis. **Thesis: most Christian readings will involve an unwillingness to interrogate the text, and will promote an exercise in the suspension and negation of its most essential literary qualities.**

DISCUSSION

To fully explore the battle lines between Christian and humanist readings you would need to read for yourself Empson's and Lewis's books about the poem. But the gist of their difference turns on the extent to which the reader should identify with the condition of Adam and Eve. If, as above, we search for some meaning in their decision to eat the fruit, are we misusing reason in just the same way as our ancestors? Lewis argued that the poem's moral of obedience has the 'desolating clarity' of what we were taught in the nursery. Children might be incapable of understanding the rules and edicts of their parents but they should realize that these apparently arbitrary regulations are the result of the latter's love for and wish to protect their offspring. Empson counters this as follows: 'A father may reasonably impose a random prohibition to test the character of his children, but anyone would agree that he should then judge an act of disobedience in the light of its intention' (1961: 161) to which Lewis, had he the opportunity, would have replied that, in this context, it is wrong to regard ourselves as the 'anyone' who might reflect upon the behaviour of another human being since this imposes a far too literal interpretation upon God the Father. He is not a human being and we should not attempt to assess His behaviour by our standards. The following is from L.A. Cormican's contribution to the *Penguin Guide to English Literature*, and it might just as easily have been written by Lewis:

> by justification Milton did not mean a merely logical demonstration which would prove an intellectual conclusion and bring God within the framework of the rational universe. He uses the word with the overtones it acquired from New Testament usage, where it implies a divine, not a human or logical understanding, a supernal illumination from the Holy Spirit . . . If the ways of God can be justified, it must be through a purification of the heart rather than by the reasonings of the intellect.   (1960: 175)

Cormican is referring to our response to a literary text, but compare his thesis with the following extract from a sermon by the clergyman and theologian Thomas Sutton, published in 1632.

> Why did God create man apt to fall? Why did hee not keepe him from falling? . . . Why doth God condemne men for unbeleefe, seeing no man can beleeve, except God confer faith upon him? . . . Is not God unjust and cruell to predestinate men . . . before they have done any evil? . . . Let us passe by curious questions, bid adieu to all vaine speculations. Let us exercise our selves in searching the scripture.[3]

The phrase that concludes the first passage, 'reasonings of the intellect', matches the second passage's reference to 'curious questions' and 'vaine speculations', but the latter, in the seventeenth-century manner, are nicely ambiguous. Our curiosity draws us to questions that are in themselves curious, and our consequent speculations are both 'vaine' (without substance) and attendant upon the vanity of readers who wish to behold and command the truth. But despite such stylistic nuances the two passages testify to the endurance of the Christian approach; the feelings of doubt and scepticism created by *Paradise Lost* should be treated in the same way as the uncertainties that will inevitably challenge the faith of the ordinary Christian. But, since the seventeenth century, Christian perceptions of the world and literary writing have themselves been challenged.

Lewis stated in *A Preface to Paradise Lost* that 'Many of those who say they dislike Milton's God only mean they dislike God' (1942: 126). If it were as simple as this we could stop this exercise now, content in our knowledge that for the Christian reader any further doubts and uncertainties about Milton's dramatization of the Fall will be resolved by their awareness of the dominant, overarching structures of scripture and faith; and equally certain that the troubling interrogations of the humanist method will find even deeper and more problematic inconsistencies and contradictions. In the rest of this chapter, I hope to show that it is not. I want you to concentrate on two related and often interwoven themes. The first is familiar; what can literature do that other forms of human expression and analysis cannot? We have seen how *Paradise Lost* sits uneasily beside its scriptural and theological counterparts and we will in due course consider its relation to other literary writing of the seventeenth century, by Milton and others. The second theme returns us to the narrative of the Fall. I have so far referred to 'their' act of disobedience, but it will be clear to you that Adam's decision to follow Eve is attended by questions and issues that I shall categorize as sexuality and sexual difference. It is at the interface between our awareness of humanity as divided by gender and the mediation of this division in literature that we might begin to see how *Paradise Lost* can address issues beyond the straightforward, and perhaps rather limiting, choice between Christian and humanist responses.

Adam, Eve and Literature

Read Book IX, lines 896–1016. What changes in Adam and Eve do you notice? What reason does Adam give for accepting the fruit from Eve? And what reason does Milton further supply?

DISCUSSION

An enormous number of events take place in this relatively short section. Adam is transformed from the content, almost naïvely content, weaver of a garland of flowers for his beloved – no doubt symbolizing her natural beauty and purity (838–44) – into someone who 'on Eve' will 'cast lascivious eyes' until before long, 'in lust they (Adam and Eve) burn' (1013–15). We have seen how

the misuse, or misunderstanding, of the gift of reason has contributed to the fall of Eve, but if Adam's own account – assisted
by Milton's third person interjections – is a reliable indicator
of motivation, his own decision is much more spontaneous and
straightforward. His one concession to serious reasoning occurs
between lines 926–951 where he reflects upon Eve's story of how
Satan appears unharmed by the act and adds his own thoughts on
how their 'creator wise' could hardly be expected to undo His
own work (and admit defeat by Satan) in His threat to 'uncreate'
them. But the much more dominant impression is that, once aware
of Eve's act, Adam has no choice but to follow her. First 'to
himself' he states,

>   I feel
> The link of nature draw me: Flesh of flesh,
> Bone of my bone thou art, and from thy state
> Mine never shall be parted, bliss or woe.
>   (913–16)

Then, to Eve,

> So forcible within my heart I feel
> The bond of nature draw me to my own,
> My own in thee, for what thou art is mine;
> Our state cannot be severed; we are one,
> One flesh; to lose thee were to lose myself.
>   (955–9)

And the episode is summed up by Milton:

> She gave him of that fair enticing fruit
> With liberal hand: he scrupled not to eat
> Against his better knowledge, not deceived
> But fondly overcome with female charm.
>   (996–9)

On the surface these three extracts seem to fit into a consistent
narrative pattern, but examine them more closely and see if there
is anything peculiar about the way in which the imagery inter-
weaves with what is actually being said. In the first two there is a
constant emphasis upon their state of physical, and it is implied
spiritual, unity: 'The link of nature', 'flesh of flesh', 'The bond of
nature', 'My own in thee', 'One flesh'. The question we should ask
ourselves is of whether Milton exploits or even distorts this
pattern of meanings in his summary. When he states that 'she gave
him of that fair enticing fruit/With liberal hand' he seems to make
use of a very subtle confluence of the literal and the figurative.
We know that even in his least corrupt state Adam admires her

beauty, and in this context the 'fair enticing fruit', so liberally offered, could just as easily refer to her own physical presence as it does to the item from the tree.

I mention these stylistic oddities because critics since Waldock have noted that Milton is being a little extravagant with authorial wisdom in his rationale of Adam's decision – 'fondly overcome with female charm'. Is Milton inserting for the reader an almost subliminal link between Adam's pattern of physical imagery, whose intent at first seems to be more figurative than lascivious, and his own unambiguous interpretation that her 'flesh', her sexual allure, is the prime motivating force in his decision to fall? Read these extracts again and see if your first impression of what Adam means is in any way affected by Milton's summary.

If there is reason to suspect Milton of manipulating the reader's responses, can this strategy be explained? Consider the narrative problems he faces. This is the turning point in the story of the Fall, after which he will no longer be troubled by the problem of presenting the unknowable in literary form. After the Fall Adam and Eve will no longer be a refractory index between the reader and the reader's perception of God – we will all share the same fallen condition. But in the meantime he faces the more difficult problem of describing how one half of pre-lapsarian humanity communicates with and responds to his post-lapsarian counterpart. Themes and narrative patterns seem capable of both collision and synthesis. After all, we already know from Book VIII lines 607–17, that Adam seems to appreciate that the love he feels for Eve (partly physical) partakes of his greater love for God (mutual and transcendent). The question of why he is shifted from a balance between the two to an obsession with the former might be resolved by pointing out that he is unequipped to transplant the theories and declarations of abstract debate into the more immediate and traumatic circumstances of losing his only companion. We can even discern a fatalistic pattern, beginning with his statement to God that he needs a partner and ending in that person becoming the cause of his disobedience – the Fall began with his creation. But despite these textual symmetries we can't help noticing that, at least according to Milton, his decision to eat the fruit is prompted by an instinct that we would more readily associate with our fallen condition, sex and fear of loneliness. Indeed their first post-original sin is a sordid echo of Milton's Book IV description of their innocent sexual liaison. One implication that we cannot ignore is that the lure of fallen woman was capable of drawing unfallen man very rapidly into a state of corruption. Adam, from what we know of him, seems less likely

to misunderstand the relationship between reason and the rule
than did his more impulsive partner, so perhaps Milton needs to
add weight to the psychological plausibility of Adam's decision by
implanting what is an unashamedly literary and social convention
– men are tempted by women.

In order to make any judgements on this we need to look more
closely at how Milton's presentation of Adam and Eve relates to
contemporary images of sexuality – literary and non-literary.

Milton and Feminist Criticism

Feminist criticism is divided in its approaches to Milton and
Paradise Lost. Charges of misogyny go back as far as Samuel
Johnson, and are generally based upon the simplistic and speculative formula that the failure of his first marriage to Mary Powell
was the motive for his divorce tracts and that these personal and
ideological commitments spilled over into his literary presentation
of women, particularly Eve. Since the early 1970s the more
sophisticated feminist critics have presented us with a number of
intriguing revisions and alternatives to this thesis. M. Landy, for
instance, has argued that the distinctive roles and characteristics
of Adam and Eve are less the consequence of Milton's own prejudices and more part of a general tendency for male dominated
social systems to establish a foundation and origin for their
current conventions of gender distinction. The argument goes
something like this: the popular conception of the male as active,
rational, public and dominant and the female as contemplative,
instinctive, domestic and subservient are justified and perpetuated
through the mythology of religion and culture. The Fall built into
traditional, particularly Roman Catholic, belief, a structural
misogyny. The hierarchy of institutionalized religion – which
would often underpin or at least mirror the domestic and social
hierarchy – was, and in many cases still is, based upon a male
dominated line of communication between human beings and
God. The rationale for such a structure draws upon the original
patterns of gendered behaviour and temperament inscribed in
the Bible: Eve caused the disaster, Adam picked up the pieces.
Paradise Lost could not alter the perceived story of our origins,
but did its literary representation of these events further sub-
stantiate traditional models of gender distinction? Think back to
Eve's first memories of existence (tentative and potentially nar-
cissistic), her duties in the Garden (domestic and culinary), and
her use of reason (intuitive and provocative), and compare these
with Adam's role as adviser, interlocutor with Raphael and,

finally, victim of female instinct. Landy would, on the face of it, seem to have a case.

Other critics such as B.K. Lewalski have argued that Milton's engagement with gender division is more pluralistic and challenging than it might first appear. For instance, Eve's insistence at the beginning of Book IX that she can cope with the Satanic threat alone can be seen as a presentation of mutual assent to sexual equality – the tragic consequences of their separation being due more to Satan's cunning that to Eve's weakness.

We do not have the space to go into a detailed analysis of feminist interpretations,[4] and I think that the best way to come to our own conclusions is to compare the Adam–Eve distinction with the dominant stereotypes of contemporary writing.

We will start with Milton. William Empson gave some attention to a comparison between Eve and Delilah of *Samson Agonistes*, but as we shall see a more intriguing correspondence emerges when we consider the only detailed representation of women of Milton's earlier writing, the Lady in his masque *Comus*. The plot of this short dramatic piece is based upon the attempt by Comus, a demonic supernatural presence, to seduce the Lady, whose lack of a specific proper name leads us to suspect that she is a personified symbol of her gender.

The most important section of *Comus* is lines 599–813. The Lady is secured in an 'enchanted chair' and is challenged by Comus's rhetorical arguments on why she should continue to preserve her virginity. To understand the significance of this beyond its function as a simple moral tale we should note that in 1634, when Comus was first performed, the genre and technique of non-dramatic poetry was dominated by the 'metaphysicals'.[5] The feature of metaphysical technique that is most relevant to our discussion is the use of the dramatic situation. The reader will effectively listen as the poet or his fictional persona creates tantalizing and usually persuasive patterns of elliptical syntax and metaphor. The speaker will use poetic devices to convince or attempt to convince the addressee of something that in ordinary circumstances would seem paradoxical, morally or philosophically inconsistent. One of the most common formulas for the amatory lyric of this school was to have the male voice address a silent female presence, very often with the intention of changing her opinion on some issue. In a number of the most popular lyrics in this genre, such as John Donne's 'The Flea' and 'The Extasie', the dominating male presence would employ his most persuasive rhetorical skills in order to convince the female that sex was not as she seems to believe, merely a sinful and hedonistic act, but something that would provide them with an experience of spiritual unity and commitment.

Consider Comus's technique of persuasion:

> If all the world
> Should in a pet of temperance feed on pulse
> Drink the clear stream, and nothing wear but frieze
> The All-giver would be unthanked, would be unpraised
> Not half his riches known, and yet despised.
>
> (720–4)

> Beauty is nature's coin, must not be hoarded,
> But must be current, and the good thereof
> Consists in mutual and partaken bliss,
> Unsavoury in the enjoyment of itself.
> If you let slip time, like a neglected rose
> It withers on the stalk with languished head.
>
> (739–44)

This reminds me of Satan's address to Eve, particularly in the first extract where Comus attempts to convince the Lady that what she denies him actually runs against God's ('the All-giver's') intention in creating the natural world. In the second extract the context shifts toward the human, temporal dimension; life is short and if we neglect our natural gifts they will decay and eventually vanish. Compare this with what is probably the best known example of the metaphysical technique of persuasion by fear, from Andrew Marvell's 'To His Coy Mistress'.

> Now therefore, while the youthful hue
> Sits on thy skin like morning dew,
> And while thy willing soul transpires
> At every pore with instant fires,
> Now let us sport us while we may,
> And now like amorous birds of prey
> Rather at once our time devour
> Than languish in his slow-chapt power.
>
> (33–40)

Comus appears to be both a subtle anticipation of Milton's later creation of Satan and a more immediate echo of the techniques and strategies of the early seventeenth-century amatory lyric. But can we find a similar network of parallels and correspondences for the Lady? First, she is unlike the addressee of the metaphysical lyric because she has the power to answer back, but we should hesitate before transposing her with Eve since she is subject to the rules and conditions of fallen humanity. What does she say? Her speech begins:

I had not thought to have unlocked my lips
In this unhallowed air, but that this juggler
Would think to charm my judgment, as mine eyes,
Obtruding false rules pranked in reason's garb.
(756–9)

She goes on to dismiss his complex rhetorical arguments, and her own defence turns upon her certainty that a belief in God's will (in this case the preservation of virginity outside marriage) cannot be overturned by linguistic subterfuge.

Thou hast not ear nor soul to apprehend
The subtle notion and high mystery
That must be uttered to unfold the sage
And serious doctrine of Virginity . . .
Enjoy your dear wit and gay rhetoric
That hath so well been taught her dazzling fence
Thou art not fit to hear thyself convinced.
(784–92)

Several intriguing patterns of significance emerge here. She seems, first of all, to be playing out the role that the reader, feminist or not, would have wished on Eve. Her argument is straightforward: 'false rules pranked in reasons garb', 'dear wit and gay rhetoric' cannot penetrate the armour of faith and the imperatives of 'serious doctrine'. The notion of a fallen woman being more fully equipped to deal with temptation and 'false rules' than her un-fallen predecessor carries the implication that the Fall, rather than being a tragedy, was a salutary lesson, a stage in the progress of humanity towards wisdom, and this concept of 'the Fortunate Fall' will be dealt with more fully in the next chapter. For the moment let us examine two, more immediate, issues.

1   The Status of a Female Literary Character

It is difficult to find a counterpart for the Lady in sixteenth- or seventeenth-century literature. She functions as an instrument in what is clearly a polemic against the assumptions and techniques of the (male) lyric presence in early seventeenth-century poetry. In a broader context she controls the plot of this drama. Comus, the rhetorician, is left powerless and the masque ends with her being rescued by her brothers. Can you think of a woman in the dramatic writing of this period who exercises a similar influence upon the narrative of her text? True, Portia in *The Merchant of Venice* resolves the legal conundrum of Shylock's agreement with Antonio, but in order to do so she has to be disguised as a man. Isabella in *Measure for Measure* pleads, with a good deal of judicial and philosophic acumen, for the life of her brother, but Angelo, the recipient of her case, ignores her wisdom and his desire for her body plunges the play in a bizarre psycho-drama of mental and sexual illusion. The Lady is the only female literary presence of the period who is capable of asserting her will and identity without either disguising her sexuality or allowing it to become part of a bargain.

We could from this argue that Milton did not use the portrayal of Eve as a means of satisfying his misogynistic prejudices, but rather that her role as the initiator of the Fall was scripturally ordained, a fact that he could not change.

The sense of the Lady as an independent, intellectually decisive figure is not contradicted by Milton's presentation of women in the divorce tracts. Indeed in the opening of the first chapter of *The Doctrine and Discipline of Divorce* he states that 'indisposition, unfitness or contrariety of mind' in the man or the woman is far more significant a cause for divorce than the usual instance of the woman's inability to bear children. Consider the following extract from his discourse *On Christian Doctrine*. How does Milton's summary of the two passages from scripture differ from what they actually say?

> Gen. iii. 6: *The woman took some of the fruit and ate it, and gave some to her husband and he ate it.* Hence I Tim. ii. 14: *Adam was not deceived, but the woman was deceived and was the cause of the transgression* . . . Anyone who examines this sin carefully will admit, and rightly, that it was a most atrocious offence, and that it broke every part of the law. For what fault is there which man did not commit in committing this sin? He was to be condemned both for trusting Satan and for not trusting God; he was faithless, ungrateful, disobedient, greedy, uxorious; she negligent of her husband's welfare; both of them committed theft, robbery with violence, murder against their children (i.e. the whole human race); each was sacrilegious and deceitful, cunningly aspiring to divinity although thoroughly unworthy of it, proud and arrogant.
>
> (Yale, VI, 1953: 383–4, original emphasis)

Is it not the case that the quotations from Genesis and Timothy, which appear to lay primary blame upon Eve, are subtly reworked by Milton into a concept of equally shared guilt – if culpability can be measured in pronoun cases we find five 'he's', one 'she' and eight 'theys'.

The question we now have to face is this. If there is sufficient evidence in Milton's other writings, not of lingering misogyny but of a tendency to regard women as social and intellectual equals, then why in *Paradise Lost* does Eve appear to be more culpable

than Adam? To address this we should move to the second issue raised by the correspondences between the Lady and Eve.

2   The Paradox of Literature

What is the essential difference between the response of the Lady to Comus and that of Eve to Satan? The difference seems to me to exist in what the former refuses to do. She, unlike Eve, does not submit herself to the codes and strategems of rhetorical, or to be more specific, poetic discourse, whose chief benefits, it is implied, are in the imposition of untruths, deceptions and distortions of fact – and we might note here that the Lady's speech resembles God's, in Book III, in the sense that both subdue any reliance upon metaphor and rhetorical play. The message seems to be that a reliance upon literary devices in addressing matters of morality, faith or Christian doctrine will inevitably obscure what ought to be a transparent evocation of truth and duty. Having come to this conclusion we must then face the paradoxical fact that *Paradise Lost* is a literary text. Think back to what Lewis said of certain humanist commentators: 'Many of those who say they dislike Milton's God only mean they dislike God.' This might seem, on the face of it, to be a rather narrow, prescriptive attitude to intelligent, free thinking methods of literary interpretation, but it could also be read as an, albeit, half-intended, complement to Milton's success in creating a text which opens itself to so many opposed and often conflicting meanings. In this light the formula could be adapted to something like 'Many of those who say they dislike the line "fondly overcome with female charm" only mean they dislike men', or even, 'Many of those who say they appreciate Milton's presentation of Eve only mean they dislike women.' *Paradise Lost* follows the biblical narrative but it also proclaims itself as a literary text. As such it challenges the reader to examine the conflict between their private idiosyncracies or beliefs – be they humanist or Christian, misogynist or feminist – and the fabulated, but very often immediate, world of the poet, his characters and their actions. Think again about the 'moral' of the correspondence between the Lady and Eve. The villain would seem to be literature, and this might strengthen the case of Christian critics such as Lewis or Cormican who would urge the reader to suspend any fugitive doubts about Christian faith that might be stirred by the poem. This may be sound advice in the broader context of preventing the modern decay of religious belief, but it also means that as literary readers, we must read the poem as 'doctrine' and suspend our awareness of a considerable amount of its effect. One of the reasons for the perpetuation of critical writing on Milton and his poem is that they are capable of raising questions in readers which, in their encounters with other literature, they might be able to suspend or marginalize. Perhaps literature is a villain, but only if it allows us to confirm our narrow prejudices without first confronting the alternatives. In a sense then, the division between the Christian and humanist readers of *Paradise Lost* is rather like that between the Lady and Eve; the former while appreciating the resources and powers of literary technique will return finally to the immutable truths of doctrine and belief. The latter will allow themselves to be drawn into the fascinating questions and paradoxes of the text and be guided only by a mixture of intuition and reason. **Is it possible to strike a balance between these two approaches which, while maintaining an allegiance to one, will not deny the validity of the other?**

DISCUSSION

Milton for all his *ex cathedra* writings on politics, society and religion is rather sparing in his instructions on what to do with literature. We have so far had to draw inferences from his other literary writings, but there is a passage in Book VIII of the poem in which Raphael seems to address the problems of perception and interpretation that are relevant to the above question.

> Which else to several spheres thou must ascribe,
> Moved contrary with thwart obliquities,
> Or save the sun his labour, and that swift
> Nocturnal and diurnal rhomb supposed,
> Invisible else above all stars, the wheel
> Of day and night; which needs not thy belief,
> If earth industrious of her self fetch day
> Travelling east, and with her part averse
> From the sun's beam meet night, her other part
> Still luminous by his ray. What if that light
> Sent from her through the wide transpicious air,
> To the terrestrial moon be as a star
> Enlightening her by day, as she by night
> This earth? Reciprocal, if land be there,
> Fields and inhabitants: her spots thou seest
> As clouds, and clouds may rain, and rain produce
> Fruits in here softened soil, for some to eat
> Allotted there; and other suns perhaps
> With their attendant moons thou wilt descry
> Communicating male and female light,
> Which two great sexes animate the world,

Stored in each orb perhaps with some that live
For such vast room in nature unpossessed
By living soul, desert and desolate,
Only to shine, yet scarce to contribute
Each orb a glimpse of light, conveyed so far
Down to this habitable, which returns
Light back to them, is obvious to dispute.
But whether thus these things, or whether not,
Whether the sun predominent in heaven
Rise on the earth, or earth rise on the sun,
He from the east his flaming road begin,
Or she from west her silent course advance
With inoffensive pace that spinning sleeps
On her soft axle, while she paces even,
And bears thee soft with the smooth air along,
Solicit not thy thoughts with matters hid,
Leave them to God above, him serve and fear;
(131–68)

I would argue that this is one of the most complex and problematic passages in the poem. Consider the different levels at which it operates. First it would involve the contemporary reader in a debate that was taking place between two of the most prominent thinkers of the period. John Wilkins, scientist, philosopher of language and co-founder of the Royal Society was a proponent of the 'new philosophy' of Copernicus and Galileo, and Alexander Ross, his opponent, was an adherent of the ancient theories of Ptolemy. The beginning of the passage and the sequence preceding it give roughly equal weight to the ideas of each thinker on the nature of the cosmos, but the substance of the debate is of less significance than the way that Raphael makes use of it.[6] His discourse, beginning at line 114, consists of a series of questions and hypotheses. This might be interpreted as a liberal gesture on Milton's part towards the equal validity of opposed contemporary theories, but consider Raphael's conclusion.

Solicit not thy thoughts with matters hid
Leave them to God above, him serve and fear;
(167–8)

If Raphael is addressing the reader as well as Adam we must assume that his advice, and Milton's, is to forego rational enquiry and empirical evidence in favour of faith and trust in the unknowable. But is he? We should remember that one of the theological tenets of the Fall, and one that Milton does not discount, is that the faults and idiosyncrasies which caused the act of disobedience would be bequeathed to us. So, although we might recognize the errors involved in soliciting our thoughts with

matters hid we should also accept that this urge to enquire is an
irrevocable part of our human condition. What Adam was advised
not to do has become, for good or ill, something we will inevitably
do. Indeed, we know that Milton himself took an active interest in
the very debate that Raphael advises Adam to ignore.

With this in mind consider what Raphael, in his concluding
hypothesis, actually surmises (131–166). This is not merely a
theory of astronomy, it is also a formula for the origins and the
innate characteristics of gender. The correspondences between
such natural polarities as the sun and the moon and the social and
intellectual manifestations of sexual difference go back to Pliny,
who claimed that the sun is a 'masculine star, burning up and
absorbing everything' while the moon is a 'feminine and delicate
planet', and this homology had been challenged by the gnostic
thesis that 'male light' is mental and intellectual and that 'female
light' is physical.[7] Milton, via Raphael, neither endorses nor
attempts to overturn any of these theories. What he does is to
expose them as essentially contrivances of the human appetite for
enquiry, analysis and categorization. In an important sense he pre-
empts the twentieth-century schools of philosophic scepticism
generally known as structuralism and poststructuralism. I'll
examine this correspondence in more detail in Chapter 5, but a
brief summary is called for. Structuralism and poststructuralism
are grounded upon the dominance of the sign in human systems of
thought and communication. The sign, be it linguistic or visual,
allows us to make sense of what would otherwise be a formless
continuum of phenomena. So when we claim to have found
connections between such objects as the sun and the moon and
patterns of behaviour that divide the male from the female we are,
according to the structuralist, imposing a system of signs upon
apparently unrelated phenomena, and as a consequence we are
able to move from empirical observation to more general theories
of how and why we exist and behave. The most problematic
implication of structuralist thinking is that the sought after goal of
a final truth, whether religious or philosophic, is something that
we might persuade ourselves that we've found, but which is in
reality something that we have constructed through our ingenious
deployment of sign systems. Milton shares this sceptical view of
the human desire to create systems of signification that will grant
us access to some ultimate, immutable truth, but he differs from
the structuralists in his certainty that although this truth, God,
exists, it is a condition of human existence that our attempts to
locate it will merely reflect our own ambitions and limitations. **But
what is his intention in foregrounding this paradoxical yet in-**

evitable relation between the desire for validation and proof and the impossible nature of such enterprises?

DISCUSSION

Let us now return to the question that prompted our excursion into Raphael's discourse – how can we hope to balance the opposing interpretive patterns of the poem, Christian or humanist, feminist or patriarchal? Think back again to the delicious irony Raphael's advice to 'Solicit not thy thoughts with matters hid'. It is ironic because the complex systems of analysis that he had dangled tantalizingly before Adam had come to represent, in the 1660s, the frontiers of philosophic and scientific enquiry. If systems of natural, sexual and psychological enquiry are seen to be self-perpetuating functions of our fallen condition, why not include in this the communicative medium which encompasses and incorporates all of these dimensions of human thought and perception but which is honest about its openness to endless and finally unresolvable interpretations? I refer to literature. Perhaps in writing *Paradise Lost*, Milton, like Raphael, is offering the reader an engagingly complex network of identifications, logical conundrums, narrative paradoxes, which will never grant us access to some final truth, but which, like the astronomical theories of Alexander Ross and John Wilkins, should be respected as the best that man can do. Looked at in this way it is possible to see how the opposing strategies of interpretation can indeed be balanced. It is a literary paradox but not one that we can disentangle and resolve. Christian readers will urge us to suspend our appetite for speculation and enquiry, but Milton, unlike his contemporary Sutton (see above p. 50) who urges us to 'passe by curious questions, bid adieu to all vaine speculations', actually obliges us to ponder and confront these issues. Humanist readers will press on further into the labyrinth of interpretive conflict and uncertainty, again with the apparent approval of Milton, who after all created the puzzle, but with the nagging possibility that the text and its creator will always be one step ahead. For every interpretation or conjecture on why Milton presented God or Eve or Raphael in a particular way there will always be an equally valid alternative.

Summary

Reaching the end of Book IX I feel that I have not so much read the poem – in the sense that reading might involve a passive, if admiring, journey through the narrative of a novel – but more that I have become involved in a struggle with something whose techniques are endlessly perplexing and whose objectives are now more intangible than they were at the beginning.

I might, in desperation, try to find a precedent for such an experience, by citing the more recent writings of modernism in which texts such as Eliot's *The Waste Land*, Pound's *Cantos* or even Joyce's *Finnegan's Wake* present themes, motifs and patterns of coherence only to draw them back into a montage of discontinuities and false conclusions. We will look more closely at such comparative exercises in the closing chapter, but for the moment let us remind ourselves of where we are. We are about to enter the concluding section of the poem, in which all of its human characters, a category which includes Milton and us, share the same condition of distance and loss. The question we should consider is of how our experience of what is to come will affect our battered perceptions of what has already occurred.

4. Outcomes and Consequences: Books X–XII

Read Books X–XII. After doing so you will have cause to reflect upon the closing propositions of the last chapter with renewed scepticism and perplexity. Our objective in this chapter will be to test the optimistic notion of the poem as a text which can accommodate divergent and contradictory impressions. The uneasy contrast between Christian and humanist perceptions, between Milton as a dogmatic promulgator of truths and Milton as the tolerant and liberal literary craftsman is by no means settled in the closing books. But are these polarities driven further apart or do we see them redeployed in a state of creative juxtaposition? Before addressing these questions we should try to draw up a diagram of the most prominent themes and developments.

Structure and Pattern

What is the main change that takes place between Books X and XI? In the former, the narrative of the Fall is continued with God observing the act of disobedience and sending the Son to pass judgement on Adam and Eve. The death sentence is deferred and they, and their offspring, are condemned to a limited tenure of earthly existence, much of it to be spent in thankless toil and sorrow (103–228). There then follows a lengthy section (228–720) in which Satan and his followers have their celebrations ruined by being turned into serpents and beset by unquenchable thirst and unassuagable appetite – so much for victory. The most important section is from 720 to the end of the book, because as we shall see this operates as a point of transformation from what Adam and Eve were to what they will become. It is the axis between the narrative of the Fall and Books XI and XII. In these the angel Michael shows Adam a vision of the future, drawn partly from the Old Testament, but bearing a close resemblance to the condition of life in seventeenth-century England.

DISCUSSION

Read lines 720–1104 of Book X. The two most significant parts of this exchange seem to me to be the suicide arguments. The first occurs in Adam's introspective soliloquy.

> But say
> That death be not one stroke as I supposed,
> Bereaving sense, but endless misery
> From this day onward, which I feel begun
> Both in me, and without me, and so last
> To perpetuity.
>
> (808–13)

He realizes that death is not something that will free him from his condition, but rather that he is carrying death around with him, and any loss of his substantial form will not necessarily be an escape from torment, 'both death and I/Am found eternal, and incorporate both,' (815–15). This realisation does not console him; it merely sustains the circling or rather the downward spiralling of his argument. At this point Eve arrives. She readily accepts blame for their condition, Adam is eventually moved by her contrition, and they comfort each other. All this has apparently fortified Adam because when Eve herself produces the suicide argument he is ready to point out its flaws. Compare Eve's proposition with Adam's.

> If care of our descent perplex us most,
> Which must be born to certain woe, devoured
> By death at last, and miserable it is
> To be to others cause of misery,
> Our own begotten, and our loins to bring
> Into this cursed world a woeful race
> That after wretched life must be at last
> Food for so foul a monster in thy power
> It lies, yet ere conception to prevent
> The race unblest, to being yet unbegot.
> Childless thou art, childless remain:
> So death shall be deceived his glut, and with us two
> Be forced to satisfy his ravenous maw.
>
> (979–91)

This provides the opportunity for Adam to exercise, in what would now appear to be the approved way, his gift of reason. He points out that death is something they cannot control, and that her suggestion of a refusal to breed would only upset the natural order, cause frustration and rancour in both of them and, most importantly, grant a final victory to Satan, who had set out to destroy them.

In one sense the reader is swept along towards the inevitable conclusion of this exchange – it is consistent with scripture, and Christian history tells us that had they decided to kill themselves neither Milton nor the reader would be around to debate their decision – but at the same time it is difficult to ignore the emotive power of Eve's proposition. She is offering to release whatever tenuous grip upon happiness they can still maintain in order to spare their offspring a promised condition of misery.

We can see that the suicide debate parallels the exchanges that took place between Adam, Eve and Raphael before the Fall. It is the second test of their use of free will and reason. But now nothing is left open to speculation or possibility. Adam knows their duty both as penitents and as parents of God's created species, and Book X ends with a narrowing of the textual focus. Read lines 1041–1096. In this he no longer ponders such absolutes as the will of God and the nature of the cosmos, and instead concentrates on more practical problems such as how they might warm themselves against the new and disagreeable climate by rubbing two sticks together.

Has emphasis shifted towards the Christian interpretive model? Adam is now able to respond correctly to his circumstances and to the will of God, because his reason has been tempered with the restraint that comes, not from any form of enlightenment, but from punishment. The troubling correspondences between Adam's and Eve's urge to speculate and enquire and the reader's very similar response to the logical and ethical conundrums of the text, seem finally to have been brought to a close. This effect finds its theological counterpart in something called 'The Paradox of the Fortunate Fall'. The notion of the fortunate fall was first considered in depth by St Augustine and there is an essay by A.O. Lovejoy that traces its history in literature and theology up to the time of *Paradise Lost*.[1] It is regarded as paradoxical because only the paradox provides human beings with the means by which we might understand it. It goes something like this: the Fall was a necessary stage in man's journey towards greater wisdom and awareness. We might challenge such a thesis by pointing out, (a) that it was not supposed to have happened or, (b) that if it is part of a plan, God was being both dishonest and unjust in claiming that man had free will. But we will then be reminded that the Fall was fortunate because it will prevent us from pursuing such querulous questionings. It certainly seems to have worked with Adam.

The problem for the reader is that if we accept that this theological concept should become interwoven with our perception of the poem, then we have also to accept that we have just read a literary account of the creation, the Fall of Man and the activities of God and Satan that we can never hope to understand. Some readers might be happy with the idea of Milton as first offering us some hope that his writings will clarify, if not resolve, our most fundamental problems of existence, and then, like some malevolent conjurer, revealing our complex patterns of sympathy, frustration and compassion as the consequences of vanity and perpetual misunderstanding. I am not.

Kenneth Muir (1955) argued that although the closing books were essential to the scriptural scheme of the poem they were 'poetically on a much lower level'. What he seems to mean, particularly in relation to XI and XII, is that there is no longer any need for Milton to generate dramatic or logical tension. The future, as disclosed to Adam by Michael, has already arrived, and few people would disagree that it is not as pleasant as it might have been.

Read Books XI and XII, and base your interpretive agenda upon two areas of comparison. First, consider the network of events that has led to the Fall. Each of the situations of distress that Adam witnesses is supposed to correspond with some kind of behavioural flaw or character trait that contributed to the first act of disobedience – in other words, the future of mankind will take the form of a series of punishments that in some way fit the original crime. Second, try to imagine Milton's perspective both upon his poem and his world. His story has come full circle to the point where he invites us to look back both at the behaviour of our ancestors, and, by implication, at how the consequences of their act manifest themselves in the more recent behaviour of seventeenth-century humans.

There are plenty of consequences to choose from. Let's start with the vision of Cain and Abel (XI 429–460). Adam is particularly distressed by this, 'sight/Of terror, foul and ugly to behold,/Horrid to think, how horrible to feel!' (463–5), because Michael has already explained how by some form of genetic inheritance, he is responsible for this spectacle of brother murdering brother. And we should remind ourselves that many of the first readers of this account had memories of brothers, sons and fathers facing one another across English battlefields.

> These two are brethren, Adam, and to come
> Out of thy loins; the unjust the just have slain,
> For envy that his brothers offering found
> From heaven acceptance; but the bloody fact
> Will be avenged, and the others faith approved.
> (455–8)

There is worse to come. After enquiring if there are not better ways to die, Adam is presented with the following.

> A lazar house it seemed, wherin were laid
> Numbers of all diseased, all maladies
> Of ghastly spasm, or racking torture, qualms
> Of heart-sick agony, all feverous kinds,
> Convulsions, epilepsies, fierce catarrhs
> Intestine stone and ulcer, colic pangs,
> Demoniac frenzy, moping melancholy
> And moon-struck madness, pining atrophy,
> Marasmus, and wide wasting pestilence,
> Dropsies, and asthmas, and joint racking rheums.
> Dire was the tossing, deep the groans, despair
> Tended the sick busiest from couch to couch;

And over them triumphant death his dart
Shook, but delayed to strike, though oft invoked
With vows, as their chief good, and final hope.
(479—93)

There is apparently a reason for showing Adam all this: 'that thou mayst know/What misery the inabstinence of Eve/Shall bring on men' (475—7). The theme of inabstinence and its rewards continues with a vision of the next generation of humanity thrown into a cycle of hedonism and self destruction mainly at the instigation of 'fair women'. And again the sense of Adam and Eve, particularly Eve, as the perpetrators of this chronicle of temptation, abuse and punishment is reiterated.

Book XI operates rather like an instrument of torture, with Adam watching the human race moving from generation to generation and disaster to disaster, the sequence alleviated only by Michael's advice that in order to escape the worst consequences of his fallen condition man should refrain from sensual pleasure and wordly ambition.

For the contemporary reader the most distressingly immediate section is the description of war (638—81) which although paying allegiance to the Old Testament and Virgil would evoke memories of when Englishmen, barely a decade earlier,

Lay siege, encamped; by battery, scale and mine,
Assaulting; others from the wall defend
With dart and javeline, stones and sulphurous fire;
On each hand slaughter and gigantic deeds.
(656—9)

The entire book is a catalogue of man's forthcoming miseries, and there seems little for the reader to do but, as Muir implies, to accept that our role has changed from active participants in the complex network of textual openings and puzzles to passive observers of what must be. But are things so simple?

First of all consider the parallel between Michael's function as the apocalyptic messenger and Raphael's role as adviser.

DISCUSSION

The most obvious difference seems to me to be the manner in which information is conveyed. Raphael shows Adam nothing. His discourse is purely linguistic and is consequently the source of discussion, enquiry and, finally it seems, misunderstanding. Michael however speaks only in order to clarify any doubts that

Adam might have regarding the precise significance of each vision – his interjections are more like footnotes than comments or instructions.

This confronts us with a problem that is closely related to the Chapter 3 discussion of 'The Paradox of Literature'. Michael makes it clear to Adam that the phenomena presented to him are, unlike the conundrums presented by Raphael, a straightforward visual record of fallen man's taste for sensual pleasure and material gain. There is no refractory index between seeing and understanding. At the end of book XII, very close to the conclusion of the poem, Adam shows that he understands this.

> How soon hath thy prediction, seer blest,
> Measured this transient world, the race of time,
> Till time stand fixed: beyond is all abyss,
> Eternity, whose end no eye can reach.
> Greatly instructed I shall hence depart,
> Greatly in peace of thought, and have my fill
> Of knowledge, what this vessel can contain;
> Beyond which was my folly to aspire.
> Henceforth I learn, that to obey is best,
> And love with fear the only God, to walk
> As in his presence, ever to observe
> His providence, and on him sole depend.
>   (553–64)

Michael answers,

> This having learned, thou hast attained the sum
> Of wisdom; hope no higher.
>   (575–6)

What exactly has Adam learned? Taking into account the distinction between Raphael's and Michael's methods of instruction it would appear that Adam, and by implication the reader, has been advised to depend more upon empiricism and tangible verification than upon the instruments of speculation and enquiry. Raphael offers him language, Michael shows him fact, and the encoded message would seem to be that we should not ponder what we do not and cannot know. More specifically, we are warned that language, the medium through which we explore uncertainties, should be used and interpreted with a good deal of caution. Look what happened when, first Adam with Raphael, and then Eve with Satan, attempted to bring about a unitary correlation between what might be and what language can make things appear to be. It fed their desire for enquiry, caused them to overreach their human limitations and led to disaster.

DISCUSSION

Where does this leave the reader of the poem? All the evidence that we have, at least from the closing books, is that the Christian readers are much closer than the humanists to Milton's intention. It seems that as we closed our discussion of Book IX we deluded ourselves by placing the poem within the liberal pluralistic context of an artwork that opens itself to diverse and contradictory patterns of response. It does indeed appear that the reader who has enjoyed the textual and philosophic puzzles of why God acts as He does, what sort of person Satan is and what really prompted Adam and Eve to eat the fruit, must now confront the undeniable similarities between what we do with the poem and what Adam and Eve did with language and reason. Their salutary lesson is also ours and we should cast aside all hopes of finding some intriguing and individually Miltonic perspective upon doctrinal truth and practice.

It is clear that some readers and critics are happy with this interpretation, but I am troubled by it for a number of reasons. First of all, the balance has been shifted so that the text is more an instrument of religious instruction than a complex literary exploration. What is the difference? The Bible, religious tracts and sermons all unashamedly use literary devices in order to make their point, but they are not literary texts. A literary text, in my view, is something that draws upon a limitless variety of non-literary codes and discourses – myth, religion, politics, fact, fantasy, opinion, ordinary commonplace language, rhetorical intensities – but it will not deploy these as a means to a particular and unquestionable end. True, we know for example that Macbeth, Shylock, Richard III, Scrooge, Fagin and Moll Flanders are all corrupt, villainous, murderous or generally at fault, but after emerging from their fictional worlds we do not find ourselves with a neat solution to the failings of humanity. Instead we emerge with a complex network of insights, new perspectives upon how human beings, driven by circumstances or innate characteristics, behave as they do. Literature, within the limits of this definition, will offer us another way of examining our condition, but complexity will not guarantee resolution. Viewed through the retrospective lens of the closing books *Paradise Lost* does not seem to satisfy these criteria. But what should we do now? The Christian reader, while admiring the craftsmanship of the artefact will be satisfied that it does not challenge doctrinal perceptions and beliefs, and the humanist reader can wander away, grumbling that it did not quite live up to expectations. Is there any way that we might bring these individuals back together and show them that the contest is not over yet?

One possible means of achieving this is to look again at the historical and personal circumstances of the poem's creation. We have already done this in relation to the civil war and contemporary presentations of women, but let us now concentrate on two related elements of Milton's life; his status and awareness of himself as a literary writer and his experience of England in perhaps its most turbulent and unsettled period.

To make any judgements on the value, or in some cases the meaning, of a writer's work, we have to be aware of the predominant techniques and aesthetic affiliations of their period. We have already encountered a major problem in constructing such a contextual plan in Chapter 2, because *Paradise Lost* was, within the relatively young tradition of English literary writing, unprecedented. But we might start by considering its position in the chronology of literary history.

The period between the closing decades of the sixteenth century and the civil war is generally regarded as the English Literary Renaissance. The era is dominated by drama — Shakespeare, Jonson, Marlowe and Webster being the figures who feature most prominently in the modern curriculum. In non-dramatic poetry the lyric writing men such as Shakespeare and Spenser gave way to the more adventurous and daring techniques of the early seventeenth-century metaphysical school, a phenomenon we have already encountered. Generalization is generally unwelcome in literary criticism, but it is possible to claim that the writing of the period is experimental. Apart from isolated figures such as Chaucer there was no fully established tradition of English literature. Classical precedent was widely acknowledged and adapted, but English and England and were not Greek or Rome, and the late sixteenth- to early seventeenth-century writers effectively laid the foundations for what would follow. Milton wrote his first poems in the 1620s and he continued to produce mainly short occasional or reflective pieces (with the exception of *Comus*) until the civil war and the Protectorate diverted his talents towards theological and political tracts. The question we should consider is to what extent Milton either absorbed or attempted to transcend the influence of his most prominent contemporaries. A final answer to this will demand a large amount of background reading, but I shall offer my thesis and allow you to test it against a number of extracts from his own and other writer's work.

In the first three decades of the seventeenth century the

structural centrepiece of dramatic and non-dramatic poetry was the conceit. The conceit is a metaphor whose components are drawn from areas of language and thought that would not normally be regarded as logically or intuitively related. Samuel Johnson summed this technique up as 'heterogeneous ideas yoked by violence together'. What he means by this will become clear after a reading of Donne's 'The Flea' in which the governing conceit is founded upon a comparison between sexual intercourse and a fleabite – the ideas, or in this case the events, are indeed heterogeneous or unrelated but the pseudo-logic of the poem binds them together in a bizarre but strangely persuasive argument. T.S. Eliot, a modernist and much more sympathetic than Johnson to metaphysical technique, rewrote the definition:

> A thought to Donne was an experience; it modified his sensibility. When a poet's mind is perfectly equipped for its work, it is constantly amalgamating disparate experience; the ordinary man's experience is chaotic, irregular, fragmentary. The latter falls in love, or reads Spinoza, and these two experiences have nothing to do with each other, or with the noise of the typewriter or the smell of cooking: in the mind of the poet these experiences are always forming new wholes.[2]

In other words, the key to metaphysical writing was its ability to merge and juxtapose images drawn from the intellectual and the physical and, very often, the spiritual and the sensual dimensions of language. The effect of such poetry was to throw the reader off balance, to make us think again about the relationship between ideas, images and events that we previously regarded as stable and distinct. This is what I meant in my use of the term experimental: there seemed to be no limits to linguistic and, by implication philosophic, adventures of this period.

Milton, in his early poetry did not forego the use of the conceit but his poems, unlike many of those of his contemporaries, finally disclose a pattern of certainty and indisputable truths.

Consider the following extracts from Milton's first major poem, 'On the Morning of Christ's Nativity'. The poem concentrates on how, in a single moment, pagan mythology was displaced by a new and enduring truth.

> The oracles are dumb,
> No voice or hideous hum
>   Runs through the arched roof in words deceiving
> Apollo from his shrine
> Can no more divine
>   With hollow shriek the steep of Delphos leaving.

No nightly trance, or breathed spell,
Inspires the pale-eyed priest from the prophetic cell.
(Stanza XIX)

This is a description of the effect upon the human world of the
birth of Christ. Pre-Christian language and philosophy have been
silenced. In this short passage Milton reveals his own view of the
status and nature of Christian writing, including poetry. It is not
that he wants to rid literature of classical allusion and technique,
quite the opposite, he sees himself as the reinterpreter of literary
history, as the man who can inform post-Renaissance poetry with
the kind of toughness and certainty that won't be found in the
linguistic excursions of poets such as Donne. Do I overread this
passage? Consider the following from stanzas I and II:

> Nature in awe of him
> Had doffed her gaudy trim
>
>   To hide her guilty front with innocent snow
> And on her naked shame
> Pollute with sinful blame
>   The saintly veil of maiden white to throw
> Confounded that her makers eyes
> Should look so near upon her foul deformities.

The whole of the first part of the poem makes one point: Nature,
which has been celebrated by poets as beautiful and awesome is,
compared with God and the unseen world, a 'foul deformity'.
Stanza VII:

> The sun himself withheld his wonted speed,
> And hid his head for shame
> As his inferior flame
>   The new-enlightened world no more should need.

The poem looks forward to *Paradise Lost*. It asks the question,
how can we be comfortable in this world when, through Adam
and Eve's disobedience, God has turned it into a hideous parody
of the harmony that existed in Eden before the Fall?

The theological points made in this poem have serious
implications for Milton's relationship with the writing of his
contemporaries. Donne, rather than regarding the natural world
as a 'foul deformity' a reminder of our temporal punishment,
incorporates it as one element of a delightful and fascinating
panorama of human perception and experience. In the following,
from 'The Extasie' Donne deploys images drawn from the spiritual and the natural world and appears to grant them a degree of
equality.

But as all several souls contain
  Mixture of things, they know not what
Love, these mixed souls doth mix again,
  And makes both one, each this and that.

A single violet transplant,
  The strength, the colour, and the size,
(All which before was poor, and scant),
  Redoubles still and multiplies.

When love, with one another so
  Interanimates two souls,
That abler soul, which thence doth flow,
  Defects of loneliness controls.

(33–44)

The beauty and harmony of a violet is regarded as an appropriate image to illustrate the phenomenon of the 'interanimation' of two souls – hardly a conjunction that Milton would have favoured, since he refers to nature as replete with 'naked shame' and 'sinful blame'.

It would seem that the message disclosed in the closing books of *Paradise Lost*, that the fallen world is a reminder of our loss and that man should limit his desire to read transcendent meanings into it, already informs Milton's poems of forty years earlier.

DISCUSSION

Let us consider another point of comparison between Milton and Donne, the poetic treatment of death. In Donne's 'The Relique' the principal conceit develops out of the speaker's wish to be buried with a 'bracelet of bright hair' wound around his wrist. This would, he believes, serve as a token of the immortal, enduring nature of their temporal relationship; and were the grave to be later reopened,

All women shall adore us, and some men;
And since at such time, miracles are sought,
I would have that age by this paper taught
What miracles we harmless lovers wrought.

(19–22)

In Donne's Holy Sonnet X he again ponders the notion of how the pleasures of temporal life might in some way transcend the decay of the body. He creates a double conceit by both personifying death and comparing it with sleep, and concludes,

One short sleep past, we wake eternally
And death shall be no more, Death thou shalt die.

Adam, in his acceptance of the cruel logic that death will be something that humans can never entirely free themselves from, would no doubt dismiss Donne's double image of death of being both like sleep and a phenomenon that can be destroyed, as an ingenious paradox, a strategy of self-deceit and consolation. Indeed in his funeral elegy to Edward King, *Lycidas*, Milton himself mocks the use of poetry as a means of postponing the uncomfortable fact that death is the end of temporal pleasure.

> Where were ye, Nymphs, when the remorseless deep
> Closed o'er the head of your loved Lycidas?
> For neither were ye playing on the steep
> Where your old bards, the famous Druids, lie,
> Nor on the shaggy top of Mona high
> Nor yet where Deva spreads her wizard stream.
> Ay me, I fondly dream,
> Had ye been there! – for what could that have done?
> (50–7)

The message is clear. The nymphs and old bards, both symbols of poetic inspiration, are of little use and relevance as the waters close over your face – what could they have done?

Donne treats death as a mysterious and fearsome phenomenon and weaves it into ingenious poetic strategies of a consolation – metaphoric excursions that could be prefaced with 'But what if...?'. Milton, both in *Lycidas* and thirty years later in his creation of Adam, does not detain himself with the hope of uncertainty. He knows what death means and how to face it.

It would be wrong to assume that Milton stood alone as the single defender of orthodox Christianity against the speculations of metaphysical poetry. Henry Vaughn and George Herbert adapted the techniques of the period to exclusively religious and spiritual themes, but there is a difference. Read Vaughan's 'The Retreat' or Herbert's 'Jordan' I and II and you will find that they use the freedom, the non-doctrinal latitude of poetic language and metaphoric invention to explore the limits of their faith. In Milton's pre-civil war verse we sense that poetry is the instrument and channel rather than the testing ground for his vision of theological and existential certainty.

Summary

Consider the problems raised by our excursion into literary history. The *Nativity Ode*, *L'Allegro*, *Il Penseroso*, *Lycidas*, *Comus* can all be seen to contain stylistic and philosophic threads that would be drawn together in *Paradise Lost*. Milton dwelt uneasily among the fashions and techniques of his early seventeenth-century contemporaries, but should we then assume that his Christian epic was simply the final realization of beliefs and allegiances that underpinned his earlier writing? No, because to treat his work in this way would also mean that we should accept the related judgement that Milton the poet was actually Milton the preacher or Milton the zealot in disguise, that after 1660 he simply returned to his pre-civil war role as the poet who knows and speaks the truth. It is difficult to accept this thesis because, between 1640 and 1660, he experienced, indeed participated in, events that would disturb and threaten anyone's certainty in anything. He returned to writing poetry, and he took with him most of the themes and questions that migrate through his earlier work, but their re-emergence in *Paradise Lost* offers us what I shall argue is the first and most complex example of literary history in collision with history.

DISCUSSION

In our shifts between distinct and opposing critical views of *Paradise Lost* have we ignored something that, in our encounters with the work of other major English writers, is an accepted fact? Shakespeare's *The Tempest*, Wordsworth's *The Prelude*, Joyce's *Ulysses* all interweave elements of the writer's personal and creative experience with more universal literary and philosophic themes. We might find it difficult to regard *Paradise Lost* as Milton's biographical epic for the simple reason that the narrative is biblical – his presence in the text is as commentator and co-ordinator and not as originator or commanding presence, and he has very few opportunities to establish a fictional alter ego amongst the cast of Old Testament characters. But think again about the correspondences between the biblical narrative and the events that had occupied two decades of Milton's personal and professional life.

The title given (by Christopher Hill) to the civil war and its aftermath is the English Revolution. He uses the term with some caution because revolution for the modern reader has gathered associations and images that were unknown and unthinkable in the seventeenth century. The major revolutions of the past two centuries – American, French, Russian, even Industrial – are essentially secular in character and ideology. Concepts of justice, equality, democracy, commerce are their driving forces and points of conflict. In the English Revolution the political and social aims of its participants were paralleled and determined by perceptions

of the will of God. The Cromwellians, even though divided by
faction and allegiance, shared a collective belief that the killing of
the king and the institution of a new and unprecedented form of
government, legislature and social hierarchy were ordained and
justified by their correct interpretation of scripture. Participants in
later upheavals such as Robespierre or Trotsky might well be able
to accept their displacement and the failure of their own objectives
as the consequences of the corruption, meglomania or ideological
mischief of others, but for men such as Milton solutions would
not be so easy to find. If the revolution in which he took part was
ordained and sanctioned by God, then why did it fail? To admit
that his ideals were wrong would in effect involve the abandon-
ment of a lifetime of belief and commitment, and to admit that
God had failed them would be unthinkable.

It is for this reason that we find difficulties in locating direct
allegorical parallels between *Paradise Lost* and seventeenth-
century history. To blame Satan/Cromwell or Satan/Charles I or
to cast doubts upon the composure and judgement of God would
have meant a descent into the secular continuum of cause, effect
and consequence that was anathema to Milton's deep rooted faith.
If there is a villain in *Paradise Lost*, a source for the poem's
complex interweavings of doubt, mistrust, temptation and failure,
it is John Milton. To use a modern formula, with which Milton
would probably not have been happy, the poem was his personal
catharsis. Each of its characters, including God, represents a
mirror image of what Milton had seen happen to his fellow
human beings over two decades of apocalyptic chaos, an experience in which he had taken an active and enthusiastic part.
But it is a cracked mirror. The poetic image can never be made to
fit the reality. More important than who, or what dimension of
humanity, these figures represent is our desire to find human
cyphers or correspondences for them. The reader of the poem will
be no more successful in finding a neat allegory for the complexities of human distress than would a contemporary thinker be
able to locate a genuine explanation for the political and moral
complexities of the civil war and its aftermath. *Paradise Lost*
pitches the reader's uncertainty at two levels. To understand the
wretched condition of contemporary humanity we will, inevitably,
attempt to trace this condition back to our origins, but what we
will find there is not an explanation but an anticipation of human
failure. Perceiving the poem in this way can help us to appreciate
what might otherwise be its anticlimatic and disappointingly
orthodox conclusion. If we look back from Book XII, from
Michael's advice to 'hope no higher', we should not, as some

Christian readers might urge, interpret his advice as a literary critical edict, and simply suspend the intriguing textual questions of why God acted as He did, of how unsuccessful was Raphael as an adviser, or of whether Adam or Eve was more culpable. These questions cannot be made to disappear and nor could the very similar questions that would trouble Milton in the 1660s, after twenty years of apparent misunderstanding, perplexity and failure. He, like Adam, would return to faith and trust in God the unknowable, but like the reader he will be unable to rid himself of a narrative that seems to possess no logic, justice or simple means of comprehension. His literary talent finally provided him with a way of preserving a very real and tragic paradox for posterity, and the fact that this phenomenon was accommodated by the biblical story of our origins was both appropriate and ironic. Ironic? Yes, because when Adam and Eve gaze back at the scene of their once happy state and resolve to face the difficult future their story is over, but for the reader of the 1660s, or perhaps the 1990s, the story has multiplied and is very often still part of our experience. The message of *Paradise Lost* is that although we might find peace, certainty and consolation in whatever our faith happens to be, we can never rid ourselves of that element of our fallen legacy that will prompt us to pursue explanations for human distress or to question the behaviour of God in these matters. For Milton these troubling uncertainties found an accomplice in his literary talents, and if we still wonder why a 300-year-old biblical adaptation can still divide and perplex commentators and theorists of our apparently post-Christian ethos we should ask ourselves if, in the following statement, Adam is speaking for the reader of the poem. He does not speak for me.

> Greatly instructed I shall hence depart,
> Greatly in peace of thought, and have my fill
> Of knowledge, what this vessel can contain;
> Beyond which was my folly to aspire.
> (557–60)

5. Criticism

We have reached the end of Book XII, but we have not finished reading the poem, because it is impossible to completely detach a text such as *Paradise Lost* from the questions, assumptions and interpretive controversies that have circled it for three centuries. **We have already seen how conflicts between Christian and humanist readers reflect and articulate the intrinsic divisions of the poem itself, and in this chapter we will expand the three-party exchange between you, me and the poem to include a formidable array of its readers who have also become its critics. We'll start by finding our bearings in critical history.**

DISCUSSION

In the century following the poem's publication emphasis was laid less upon what Milton wrote and more upon the way he wrote it. Dryden, Pope and Johnson seem to follow the example set in Marvell's dedicatory poem and concentrate on how successfully Milton has realized his apparent objective of creating a new and unprecedented style to accommodate the awesome grandeur of his story. Joseph Addison stands out as a critic willing to consider the uncomfortable presence of biblical figures within what he called a pagan (i.e. pre-Christian, classical) genre, but his *Spectator* essays leave the reader in no doubt that God is not diminished by this treatment nor Satan elevated to the heroic.[1]

   The question we should ask ourselves is what caused the enormous change in emphasis at the beginning of the nineteenth century. The change is undeniable.

> The reason Milton wrote in fetters when he wrote of Angels and God, and at liberty when of Devils and Hell, is because he was a true poet and of the Devil's party without knowing it.   Blake (1790)

> But around this character [Satan] he has thrown a singularity of daring, a grandeur of sufferance, and a ruined splendour, which constitute the very height of poetic sublimity.   Coleridge (1818)

> Milton's devil as a moral being is as far superior to his God, as one who perseveres to some purpose which he has conceived to be excellent, in spite of adversity or torture, is to one who in the cold security of undoubted triumph inflicts the most terrible revenge upon his enemy, not from any mistaken notion of inducing him to repent of any perseverence in enmity, but with the alleged design of exasperating him to new torments.   Shelley (1819)[2]

One reason for the tendency of the Romantics to read the poem outside its doctrinal sources could be that their perceptions of art and literature were interwoven with their perceptions of revolution, particularly those in America and France. The phenomenon of a suppressed people urged by iconoclastic free thinkers to overthrow oppressive autocracies would find very few precedents in literature or myth. So, with a few adjustments and a convenient marginalization of Milton's adherence to Christian faith, the narrative of *Paradise Lost* could be made to resemble an allegory, a prediction of what, a century later, would happen to Western politics and consciousness. C.S. Lewis makes this point, and argues that the Romantics were initiators of the trend towards sceptical, humanist readings in modern academic criticism.

> But *Paradise Lost* records a real, irreversible, unrepeatable process in the history of the universe ... The truth and passion of the presentation are unassailable. They were never, in essence, assailed until rebellion and pride came, in the romantic age, to be admired for their own sake. On this side the adverse criticism of Milton is not so much a literary phenomenon as the shadow cast upon literature by revolutionary politics, antinomian ethics, and the worship of Man by Man. After Blake, Milton criticism is lost in misunderstanding.
> Lewis (1942: 133)

Lewis's thesis that we will often carry our own ideological and subjective language with us into a reading of a text must be accepted, but what of his attendent claim that the poem records something irreversible *and* unrepeatable? Leaving aside the Romantics, can we really conclude that the patterns of behaviour and action of the poem correspond only to scripture and are coincidentally related to England in the mid-seventeenth century? I think that it is possible to identify a middle ground between Lewis and the Romantics by looking again at the biographical reading with which we closed Chapter 4. To conclude that Milton was of the devil's party without knowing it means that we will read the poem within Blake's individualistic and often bizarre perceptions

of the world, but we should not reject the possibility that Milton
had supplemented and consequently distorted the biblical narrative by deliberately blending the monoliths of the Old Testament
with very real and immediate experiences of human ambition,
misbehaviour and, it cannot be denied, heroism. Empson, Lewis's
principal adversary, makes this point very persuasively.

> The recent controversy about the poem, on the other hand, has
> largely been conducted between attackers who find it bad because it
> makes God bad and defenders who find it all right because it leaves
> God tolerable, even though Milton is tactless about him. Surely this
> is an absurd spectacle; the poem is not good in spite of but especially
> because of its moral confusions, which ought to be clear in your
> mind when you are feeling its power. I think it horrible and won-
> derful; I regard it as like Aztec or Benin sculpture, or to come nearer
> home the novels of Kafka, and am rather suspicious of any critic
> who claims not to feel anything so obvious.   (p. 13)

Empson urges the reader not to forget the poem's parallels with
scripture and faith, as the Romantics seem to do, but to regard
these as secondary to the manner in which Milton effectively
rewrites them within the very human experience of 'moral con-
fusions', the 'horrible and wonderful'. This would be consistent
with our thoughts at the close of Chapter 3, that Milton has
deliberately set up a tension between the certainties of belief and
the anarchy of experience.

The critics encountered so far might not seem to have a great
deal in common in their perceptions of the poem's true meaning
and intention, but can we discern what might be called a con-
sistency in their disagreements?

Empson's comparison of the poem with the novels of Kafka is
intriguing. Kafka's technique is essentially modernist in the sense
that his novels raise fundamental questions regarding the source
and meaning of human distress but leave the reader to contem-
plate a void of existential chaos and hopelessness. The problem
raised by the comparison is of whether Milton had really anticipated this literary trend or whether its presence provides modern
critics with a convenient category into which they might at last fit
Milton's troubling work? The former possibility must remain
open to speculation, but the latter might enable us to understand
the reason for the curious shifts in opinion on what he did and
how well he did it. The Romantics read the poem through the
refractory lens of their own beliefs and allegiances so why should
we not assume that modern critics will find their interpretations
conditioned, consciously or otherwise, by twentieth-century
perceptions of aesthetics and reality?

F.R. Leavis and T.S. Eliot are two of the most prominent and influential figures in twentieth-century literature and literary criticism. Their opinions differed on many things but on *Paradise Lost* they have come to be regarded as the founders of the modern 'anti-Miltonist' school. Their essays (Leavis, 1933; Eliot, 1936 and 1947) are focused on Milton's style, but this emerges as only one dimension of a more serious charge that he sent English poetry in the wrong direction. Eliot is politely ambivalent:

> The remoteness of Milton's verse from ordinary speech, his invention of his own poetic language, seems to me one of the marks of his greatness. [1947] [But], A disadvantage of the rhetorical style appears to be, that a dislocation takes place, through the hypertrophy of the auditory imagination at the expense of the visual and the tactile, so that the inner meaning is separated from the surface, and so tends to become something occult, or at least without effect upon the reader until fully understood.   Eliot (1936)

> It needs no unusual sensitiveness to language to perceive that, in this Grand Style, the medium calls pervasively for a kind of attention, compels an attitude towards itself, that is incompatible with sharp concrete realisation.   Leavis (1936)[3]

Both critics concentrate upon a question that we have already considered in Chapter 1. Does Milton's innovative, unprecedented style allow his characters to establish individual identities, or does it enable him to control and determine the reader's perceptions? They find in favour of the latter, but as we have seen there is a good deal of evidence – particularly in the stylistic individuality of Eve and God – to support the former. Whether or not you agree with Eliot and Leavis is up to you, and the most respected defence of Milton's technique will be found in Christopher Ricks's *Milton's Grand Style* (1963). Ricks is a master of the technique of close-reading, and he shows us how Milton succeeds in balancing a bewildering variety of localized stylistic intricacies against the broader narrative pattern. He reads it as a modern poem and his book (like Empson's) represents an important contribution to the pro-Milton school that, through the fifties and sixties, set about overturning the scepticism of the previous two decades – the earlier period being dominated by Leavis, Eliot and Lewis.

These arguments lead us to another, far more complex, question. How is it that Milton's reputation can be subjected to so many varied and often conflicting judgements? We have concentrated on the Christian versus the humanist approach, but clearly Leavis and Eliot demonstrate that our opinions can be affected by issues separate from our personal religious beliefs. No major writer, Shakespeare included, is immune from critical scepticism

but few, if any, have achieved Milton's position between ador-
ation and scorn.

One reason for this, in my opinion, is that Milton simply does
not fit into the received and accepted categories of literary history
and genre. If I were to select, more or less at random, a number of
writers judged by general consensus to be 'major', it would not be
too difficult to construct a social, historical and aesthetic context
for their work. Eliot is a modernist poet, Wordsworth is his
Romantic counterpart, Donne is the most prominent practitioner
of metaphysical poetry, Pope is the exemplary Augustan, Dickens
the most-read Victorian novelist. But what is Milton? We know
that he is a seventeenth-century writer but, as we have seen, his
work does not rest easily alongside that of his pre-civil war
contemporaries. After the Restoration the mood and technique of
poetic writing shifted toward the public, satirical poem, with
Dryden as its most celebrated practitioner, but again Milton's
later work, *Paradise Lost, Paradise Regained, Samson Agonistes*,
does not appear to have much, if anything, in common with the
trend towards political and social satire. Nor is it possible to claim
that he founded or instituted a particular tradition. It is true that
non-dramatic blank verse and its stylistic patterns became, after
Paradise Lost, an accepted convention of non-dramatic poetry,
and we will find echoes both of Milton's technique and his existential questionings in poets as diverse as Pope and Blake, but
Paradise Lost remains as a phenomenon that deserves the adjective 'unique'. Even when poets as otherwise distinct as Thomson,
Wordsworth and Tennyson wrote in blank verse they did not
merely engage with an abstract metrical code. They found themselves acknowledging and often following an idiom, a style that is
essentially Miltonic. With *Paradise Lost* Milton inscribed his
signature within the English poetic tradition, and this mark could
never be fully detached from the memory of a single text which
engages with religious and secular themes, draws its narratives
from the Bible and from contemporary experience, pays allegiance
to the classical epic, yet claims to be unprecedented.

The effect of this sense of distance from any general technique
or shared code of aesthetic affiliation is uncomfortable, because it
is always useful to find a counterpart, a point of comparison
against which we might stabilize our judgements of a writer's
contribution in their particular creative field: Donne and Herbert,
Dryden and Pope, Wordsworth and Coleridge, Eliot and Pound,
Milton and . . . ? This problem of where exactly to put Milton
among the panoply of literary greats is a constant, if usually
unacknowledged, concern in critical writing, and for the rest of

this chapter I want you to try an experiment. Let us assume that critics and poets will approach *Paradise Lost* with their own framework of allegiances and diagram of literary history. From what we have just surmised regarding the poet and his poem's relation to other texts and trends, they will face a number of difficulties; they cannot really judge him against other poets within the same literary-historical, or aesthetic field or consider his eminence in relation to the virtually non-existent tradition of the Christian epic. What they are obliged to do is to test their perceptions of his poem against the broader and more universal concepts of what literature is and should do. So let us examine the way in which *Paradise Lost* might challenge a number of the more recent theories of the identity and value of literature. We will start with its effect on poets.

Eliot's 1921 essay on 'The Metaphysical Poets' is regarded as one of the most influential modern appraisals of that school of poetry. Eliot praises the adventurous, often disorientating, use of metaphor by these poets, and the implication seems to be that he regards them as the true precursors of the equally experimental poetics of modernism. He states that after the civil war a 'dissociation of sensibility set in, from which we have never recovered, and this dissociation, as is natural, was aggravated by the influence of the two most powerful poets of the century, Milton and Dryden'.[4] What he means by this should already be evident from our own comparison between Milton and his early contemporaries: Donne speculated, surmised and perplexed, Milton knew. Milton's sensibility was dissociated because he seemed unwilling to allow literary writing to disclose or promote mysterious and uncertain associations between phenomena and absolute truth. So perhaps Eliot's apparently dispassionate and objective judgements of Milton's style are really fuelled by a more personal objection to his presence as a poet who used literature to promote a specific code of life and art – one that did not suit Eliot's own perception of what poetry ought to be and do. Harold Bloom, in the title of his 1973 book, judges Milton's effect on later poets as causing *The Anxiety of Influence*. Milton as the author of *Paradise Lost* offers his poetic successors an example and, more significantly, a challenge. His poem addresses questions of, well, everything. So they must either submit to the dominance of Milton's explanation of human existence, or they must deliberately and creatively 'misread' it in order to make room for their own contributions to art and life. The anxiety to which Bloom refers is due primarily to Milton's individuality. Dryden's *Absalom and Achitophel* (1681) is, like *Paradise Lost*, an interpolation of a biblical narrative with contemporary politics, and in it we sense Dryden's discomfort in having to work within the shadow of Milton's all-encompassing monolith. The Romantics, Coleridge, Wordsworth, Keats, Shelley and pre-eminently Blake, all attempted to interweave contemporary perceptions of the world with mythical and biblical themes, but in an important sense their freedom to command this vast cultural and philosophical framework is limited by the presence, not of a tradition, but of a single poet who had already established the terms and conditions in which such an enterprise must be conducted. By 1921 Eliot had become one of the standard bearers for the new aesthetic of modernism, and he took it upon himself to compare and contrast the new with the old, but Milton would not fit easily into distinct historical and aesthetic categories that constituted pre-twentieth-century literary history. His presence was felt by everyone, be they Augustans or Romantics, religious or secular writers. Thus we find Eliot caught in an interpretive trap; stating on the one hand that Milton's verse is 'remote' from 'ordinary speech', 'the inner meaning is separated from the surface' and on the other that he shares Dryden's guilt in plunging English poetry into the flat, pedagogic certainties of the 'dissociation of sensibility'. He could hardly do both, but Eliot, like his contemporary, Leavis, found himself dealing with a poet who refused to fit into the categories of literary history through which modern critics and poets judged their precursors. Milton's effect upon English poetic writing can best be described as disorientating. *Paradise Lost* preys upon our literary instincts; it leads us along tracks of speculation and uncertainty, its style is challenging and inventive. Yet beneath this perplexing artefact we always sense the presence of its creator, inviting us to challenge the encoded truth of the text but waiting to diffuse and pre-empt this challenge. The effect of such a text upon poets causes, as Bloom argues, a sense of anxiety. It poses difficult questions: Can this effect be repeated? If so, will we as poets find ourselves merely validating rather than transcending Milton's achievements? Its effect upon academic critics is, as we shall see, equally disorientating.

Contemporary Literary Theory

Critical schools and affiliations will very often offer us different interpretive perceptions of the same text, but it is difficult to identify a text that turns difference into conflict in quite the same way as *Paradise Lost*. Critics, like poets, will never remain immune from their own aesthetic and ideological prejudices, but it is almost as though *Paradise Lost* were specifically designed to draw out and challenge these a priori conditions.

Christian versus humanist has been the primary conflict, but how has the poem been dealt with by the more recent interdisciplinary trends in critical theory? Since the 1960s modern literary criticism, at least in its academic mode, has undergone what must arguably be its most turbulent and perplexing period. The repertoire of critical theories and practices now almost outnumbers its counterparts in literary genres. There are structuralists, post-structuralists, psychoanalytic critics, Marxists, reader-response theorists, feminists, proponents of new historicism and very often individuals who espouse two or more of these distinct interpretive categories. To decode and assess all of these forms of analysis and relate them to Milton's poem would require another book, so I shall do my best to locate the points at which *Paradise Lost* and current critical theory seem to me to interact.

At the top of the new critical hierarchy are structuralism and its close relation poststructuralism, and one could argue that a single assumption lies at the heart of structuralist thinking: Structuralism holds that an author is only partly in control of the signifiying potential of a text. He or she will inevitably surrender an element of their intention to the structure within which their text operates. The origins of this claim can be traced to the linguistic theory of Ferdinand de Saussure. Roughly summarized, Saussure argued that the linguistic system, the *langue* (grammar, syntax, words, phonemes) is what allows us to make a statement, the *parole*. Thus the notion of originality is challenged by the autonomy of the system that will limit and determine each apparently original statement. Structuralists and semioticians have extended this model beyond language to encompass the whole network of social, political and cultural sign systems. Everything – be it a work of art, a motor car, an item of clothing – can be explained in terms of the sign system within which it functions. Marxism, psychoanalysis and feminism although differing in many respects from the science of semiotics can be regarded as sharing the underlying assumption of structuralism that an event, a statement, or in this case a literary text, will be determined as much by its context as it will by the single intention of its initiator. Context or structure (hence, 'structuralism') conditions and 'explains' the meaning of the event or the text.[5]

We have already encountered versions of this argument in Christopher Hill's Marxist theory and in a variety of feminist approaches. Hill claims that we should not regard *Paradise Lost* only as a Christian epic, but as a complex allegory that dra-

matizes, without resolving, Milton's uneasy position between
orthodox puritanism and the more militant political trends of the
post-civil war period. The feminists also advise us to look behind
to biblical narrative, and to consider Milton's presentation of
gender distinction in relation to the patriachal structures of
seventeenth-century society and literature. Both interpretive
approaches share the assumption that text and author should be
examined not merely as message and messenger but rather as
components of a much broader structure within which issues such
as theology and abstract philosophy will never remain immune
from social, political and ideological beliefs and perceptions of
gendered determinism. Psychoanalytic critics, particularly those
of the traditional Freudian type, will claim that certain patterns
of narrative and imagery will disclose conflicts and obsessions
within the author's unconscious that will be suppressed by the
conventions of ordinary social discourse – Swift's apparent
concern with anality in his poems and *Gulliver's Travels* is the
classic case.

**The question we have to address is whether there is any justi-
fication for reading *Paradise Lost* as a text within and perhaps
determined by a structure. One might take the cynical view that
for readers who insist that for every literary problem there must
be a solution, structuralism in its many manifestations is all that is
left. The more traditional readers, from the Romantics to the
Christian versus humanist controversies of this century, find
themselves split between very different perceptions of what Milton
really intended, so perhaps a reading grounded upon the premise
that Milton was not entirely sure of what his poem would mean
would at least re-establish the critic as the source of new disclosures. Let us attempt a test case.**

DISCUSSION

It is not possible to locate a single passage that operates as a point
of conflict or harmony between different interpretive schools.
However, the passage quoted below will provide us with a useful
testing ground both for the validity of these different approaches
and for our own judgements as readers of the text and of its
critics. It is a description of Satan's first sight of Paradise (Book
IV). Having read the poem you will be familiar with its textual
context. What I shall do is to broaden this and examine how the
problems it raises for the reader would be dealt with by practi-
tioners of different interpretive codes. As we shall see there is a

single disagreement that splits the critical world down the middle, between those who perceive Milton as inscribed within a broader network of cultural, political, sexual and psychological codes and those who regard him as an individual who is capable of stepping outside and effectively controlling these same overarching patterns of allegiance, behaviour and belief.

> So on he fares, and to the border comes,
> Of Eden, where delicious Paradise,
> Now nearer, crowns with her enclosure green,
> As with a rural mound the champaign head
> Of a steep wilderness, whose hairy sides
> With thicket overgrown, grotesque and wild
> Access denied;
>
> (IV, 131–7)

Beneath the literal description of natural phenomena there would seem to be a subtext that invites the reader to recognize the outline of female genitalia, and indeed it was a recognized convention of sixteenth- and seventeenth- century poetry to compare the female body with a rural landscape (see Marvell's 'To His Coy Mistress'). There are a number of ways of interpreting this, all of which depend upon our judgement of whether Milton controls or is to some degree controlled by structures within and beyond the text.

A reader familiar with classical Freudian technique might interpret the subtext as the involuntary release of otherwise repressed sexual complexes. Freud writes (1972), 'The creative writer does the same as the child at play. He creates a world of fantasy which he takes very seriously – that is which he invests with large amounts of emotion – while separating it sharply from reality'. So Satan's vision is partly Milton's and it is directed toward the mother of the human race. But can we be expected to believe that this complex and admirably skilful interweaving of bucolic and sexual images is an involuntary release of sublimated Oedipal tensions? William Kerrigan in his excellent study *The Sacred Complex* (1983) revises his earlier interpretation (*The Prophetic Milton*, 1974) and argues that Milton effectively pre-empted rather than embodied the Freudian notion of the Oedipus Complex: that he was consciously aware that patterns such as sexual attraction of son to mother are part of the condition of fallen man to the extent that they will become interwoven with perceptions of our origins. Kerrigan claims, quite plausibly, that the relations between God, the Son, Satan and Eve can never remain immune from the dominant models of sexuality and the

family through which we respond to and classify human beings.
So, when we recognize the mother of humanity as causing a mildly
erotic sensation in Satan our sense of unease is supplemented by
our awareness that for us, abstracts such as innocence (Eve) and
corruption (Satan) can never remain immune from the primal
urges and instincts that have become part of our fallen legacy.
Kerrigan follows Stanley Fish in asserting that the uncomfortable
and often guilty sense of recognition that attends our encounters
with all of the characters of the poem is a deliberate strategy on
Milton's part. 'Milton's method is to recreate in the mind of the
reader the drama of the Fall, to make him fall again as Adam did'
(Fish 1967: 1). Kerrigan expands on this thesis and claims that
Milton forces us to interpose our own psychological-sexual
anxieties with the story of the creative and self-destructive forces
that brought us into existence. The point to be made about such a
reading is that it grants Milton a degree of awareness and control
that the classical Freudian reader will often deny the author. I
would side with Kerrigan's implication that Milton, far from
being the subject of a psychoanalytic reading, effectively subjects
the reader to the complex interweavings of sublimated desire
and uneasy disclosure that would have to wait for more than
two centuries for their formal designations in the works and of
methodology of Freud. But if we accept that the effect of the
passage is deliberate and contrived, what is its broader intention?
Here we should return to Stanley Fish. Consider Fish's interpretation of what happens later in Book IV (pp. 100–01).

> the Fiend
> Saw undelighted all delight, all kind
> Of living Creatures new to sight and strange:
> Two of far nobler shape
>
> (IV, 285–8)

Nobler than what or whom? Strange and new to whom? The questions may seem unnecessary in view of the narrative situation: the
creatures are new to Satan, and among them Adam and Eve stand
out 'erect and tall'. But in fact it is the reader in addition to Satan
who is the stranger in Paradise, although he may not realise it until
the description of Eve presents a problem he can solve only at his
own expense:

> She as a veil down to the slender waist
> Her unadorned golden tresses wore
> Dishevell'd, but in wanton ringlets wav'd
> As the Vine curls her tendrils, which implied
> Subjection.
>
> (IV, 304–8)

Fish goes on to argue that Milton has led the reader into a

cunningly laid trap. We, like Satan, are strangers in Paradise, and we are obliged to acknowledge this by conceding that the terms 'dishevell'd' and 'wanton' reflect our post-lapsarian condition; we cannot witness female beauty without carrying elements of corruption and eroticism into this experience. At this point in the narrative of the Fall we could hardly regard Eve as either wanton or dishevelled, but we cannot prevent ourselves from imposing our corrupt state of mind upon a lost condition of pure innocence. Read back to the quote with which we began. Satan at that point had not encountered any form of humanity, let alone its female dimension. Perhaps our sense of collusion with Satan is even more disturbing than we first imagined. The reader, in responding to Milton's double pattern of images, is thus confirmed in his state of corruption by effectively pre-empting Satan's lascivious designs. Fish again:

> The relationship between the reader and the vocabulary of Paradise is one aspect of his relationship with its inhabitants. Just as the fallen consciousness infects language, so does it make the unfallen consciousness the mirror of itself . . . Fallen man's perceptual equipment, physical and moral, is his prison; any communication from a world beyond the one he has made for himself reaches him only after it has passed through the distortions of his darkened glass.
>
> (pp. 103–4)

Fish's case, that Milton draws us into a state of uneasy recognition of our fallen condition, would seem to be more powerful than the alternative argument that he merely submits to the overarching structures of the subconscious and contemporary sexual convention. But here we face a more difficult interpretive problem. Would a woman respond to this delicately contrived exercise in response and awareness in the same way as a man? The entire framework of the reader–text relationship that underpins this debate is grounded upon the pattern of reader, text and medium (Satan) as being governed by male instincts and conventions. Fish's broader argument that the poem is designed to encourage a recognition of guilt and limitation should perhaps be qualified by the fact that the perceptual focus upon these events is primarily male. The Fall is initiated by Eve (female), but our perceptions of it are structured around the more dominant imperatives of desire and domination, shared both by Adam and Satan (male). We have already found in Chapter 3 that Milton's representations of female sexuality are not as conventionally partiarchal as they first might seem, but Fish, indirectly, raises another problem by shifting the interpretive centre away from the text and towards the relationship between the text and the reader. Sandra Gilbert in a ground-breaking article, 'Patriarchal Poetry and Women Readers:

Reflections on Milton's Bogey' (1978) takes up this issue and
conducts a reading of the poem based upon the way that women
readers perceive the relation between gender and narrative. She
argues that the exchanges that take place between Eve and the
other characters, primarily Adam of course, are overshadowed by
a sense of her having formed 'a bond with the fiend' that is
strengthened by her 'resemblance' to Sin, '(Satan's) female
avatar and the only other female who graces (or rather disgraces)
Paradise Lost' (p. 373). So when I state that 'we' perceive a
double pattern of sexual and bucolic images in our test passage I
am conveniently forgetting that this collective pronoun is split
between male readers whose deep-rooted patriachal prejudices
and assumptions will not be at all shocked by a perception of the
female as provoking lust (and in a broader sense Sin), and the
female reader whose sense of what Fish terms 'recognition' might
be more accurately described as a depressing confirmation of her
conventional status as the deviant, provocative element of the
natural order. Consider the following extract from Gilbert's essay:

> In a patriarchal Christian context the pagan goddess Wisdom may,
> Milton suggests, become the loathsome demoness Sin, for the in-
> telligence of heaven is made up exclusively of 'Spirits Masculine' and
> woman like her dark double Sin, is a 'fair defect/Of Nature' (X,
> 891–92) . . . for sensitive female readers brought up in the bosom of
> a 'masculinist', patristic, neo Manichean church, the latent as well as
> the manifest content of such a powerful work as *Paradise Lost* was
> (and is) bruisingly real. To women the unholy trinity of Satan, Sin
> and Eve, diabolically mimicking the holy trinity of God, Christ and
> Adam, must have seemed even in the 18th and 19th centuries to
> illustrate [the] historical dispossession and degradation of the female
> principle.   (pp. 373–4)

The second part of this extract posits a new relation between text
and structure. The structure in this case is the literary canon,
which plays its own part in sustaining and promoting the broader
patriarchal perceptions of what women are and how they behave.
According to Gilbert the notion of *Paradise Lost* as a dominant,
even threatening, cultural monolith (see Bloom above p. 85) finds
its counterpart in the poem's effect upon women readers and,
more significantly, women writers. She argues that the poem
remained largely unchallenged in its presentation of the creative
archetypes for male and female characteristics up to the beginning
of the twentieth century. Women writers of the nineteenth and
twentieth centuries, (Gilbert emphasizes the work of the Brontës
and Virginia Woolf), found themselves dealing not only with the
non-literary social codes of gender stereotyping but also with a
literary text which claims to describe the origins of these socio-

cultural patterns. The broader question raised by Gilbert, of what effect male writers have upon their female counterparts, is far too complex to be given proper consideration here, but we should consider the implications of her thesis for our earlier discussions of feminist criticism. We found that Milton's alleged misogyny in *Paradise Lost* was balanced both by his other literary and non-literary writing and by the fact that he was dealing with a pre-existent narrative – however he felt about the treatment or representation of women he could hardly rewrite the Old Testament. But Gilbert argues that in his overlaying of the biblical narrative with more emotive, essentially literary strategies he created a cultural precedent which placed restraints upon the way that women would come to perceive and represent themselves. He could not change scripture, but in transferring it to a different genre he installed Eve as an axis between the fictional woman who just happens to be vulnerable, impulsive and provocative and the patriarchal conception of all women as maintaining and embodying the behavioural tendencies of their prototype.

To make any judgement on this issue would involve a comparative study of *Paradise Lost* and a vast number of other literary texts. Please proceed. You will be helped in this awesome task by a number of essays that have followed Gilbert's, particularly J.M. Webber's 'The Politics of Poetry: Feminism and *Paradise Lost*' and two books by K.M. Rogers and D.K. McColley.[6]

For the moment let us return to the much broader theoretical problem of how we relate text to context (either its immediate social-political context or its ahistorical position within the literary canon). Christopher Hill in *Milton and the English Revolution* finds himself caught between the impersonal discipline of Marxist historicism and the more problematic experience of a writer who might have deliberately reshaped and distorted events in accordance with his own perceptions of them.

> *Paradise Lost* is a poem, not a historical document. The surface meaning is not necessarily to be taken at its face value, as though it were a series of statements in prose . . . But *Paradise Lost* should not be taken out of history. It is possible simply by 'reading the poem' to find in it meanings which seem unlikely to have been consciously intended by Milton . . . Our problem is to decide whether Milton *had* intentions other than his professed aim of justifying the ways of God to men.   (Hill 1977: 354)

Hill foregrounds the problem that lies at the heart of every critic's encounter with the poem. We might suspect that it is as much about Charles I and Cromwell as it is about God, that it presents Milton with the opportunity to disclose his doubts about orthodox Christian belief or that it allows him to give vent to misogynistic prejudices under the disguise of a biblical narrative. But how do we go about proving our own feelings or interpretive instincts to be valid? His method is to take us on a tour of the poem's fugitive contexts; its relation to post-civil war politics, its affirmation of unchallengeable faith, and its destiny as a sounding board for whatever political or cultural allegiance later readers (particularly the Romantics) might wish to illustrate or justify. His conclusion is that Milton deliberately, and with admirable foresight, placed his poem at the point where the universal, timeless experience of revolution, ambition, shaken belief and human failure intersect with the more immediate circumstances of late seventeenth-century England. Adam, as he departs in Book XII to face the disagreeable future is everyman, the first inhabitant of the fallen condition, but he is also John Milton left facing a very similar removal from the political paradise of the English Revolution.

> The true Paradise is to be found within, on earth, as the radical tradition had taught. Meanwhile the struggle must go on, but it is longer, soberer, less exhilerating than the heady days of *Areopagitica* or the *Defensio*. It had been bitter for Milton to come down from the heights of 1644 and 1649–50 to the trivialities and dissensions of 1659–60. It was a story to be repeated after every great revolution. Milton gritted his teeth to face the worse.   (p. 390)

Thus, according to Hill, the poem encodes a double allegory; it presents us with the universal Christian orthodoxy of the return to faith in the face of adversity, and it also carries the more direct political message that Milton had not abandoned all hope of returning to the radical Eden of the Cromwellian republic. So the poem is both an ahistorical religious document and a cunningly disguised political statement. Hill's thesis is well supported by his skill as a historian, but as to whether his use of contextual detail fully justifies his conclusion you must make your own judgements; read his book.

Let us now return to the problem of how to stabilize the poem's slide between different interpretive contexts and struc-tures. Hill, Kerrigan, Fish and Gilbert might seem to offer us different analytical priorities, but they are all obliged to concede that Milton the poet had raised problems of social, philosophic and existential instability that would not be fully engaged with in non-literary discourse for two centuries. In other words, rather than presenting material for Marxists, psychoanalysts and feminists to analyse, he effectively pre-empted their interpretive agenda. It would not be until this century that we would find the tools and the methodology to deal with the complex interweavings of philosophy, political and religious belief, sexuality, language; but perhaps Milton had got there first. *Paradise Lost* offers us enticing glimpses of each of these categories of behaviour and analysis but once we attempt to follow one of them towards a solution we find ourselves dealing with a labyrinthine puzzle in which one is never entirely separable from the other. Milton and his poem transcend the category of the analysed to become active and inexhaustible participants in the process of analysis. Is this possible? To test my thesis let us consider *Paradise Lost* in relation to the most complex and disturbing branch of poststructuralist thought.

Deconstruction

Deconstruction is an extension of the linguistic theories of Ferdinand de Saussure. Saussure argued that language is not so much a medium that enables us to reflect reality but more an autonomous structure of relations through which to some extent we construct reality. For instance the panorama of colours from, in English, blue to grey is divided very differently in Welsh and French. Do the Welsh, the French and the English see things differently or, as Saussure argues, do our different language systems impose different perceptual frameworks upon us? Jacques Derrida pursued the more disturbing implications of this concept of language as refractory system rather than transparent medium and founded the technique of deconstruction. Deconstructionists believe that language determines the limits and the structure of our temporal and spiritual awareness. God is a word, a signifier that we understand and, indeed, worship not because of its verifiable relation to a tangible entity (who has seen God?) but because it is the nexus, the meeting point of other words and concepts. God is omnipotent, omniscient, benevolent yet finally unknowable. He is the synthesis and summation of a continuum of signifiers and concepts whose validity depends upon their relation to other signifiers and concepts. We understand good because we also understand evil, and we can embody these abstract ideas in presences such as God and Satan. To deconstruct a text is to demonstrate how it subverts its own claim to reflect or mediate prelinguistic reality, to show how it creates an artificial or fictional pattern of reality by relying upon the differential structure of language. *Paradise Lost* would appear to be the archetypal self-deconstructive text (see Mary Nyquist and Geoffrey Hartman).[7] Because of the complexity of deconstructive reading, it would be unwise to try to illustrate this statement with a quote, but consider the following. *Paradise Lost* will 'justify the ways of God to men' yet at the same time it will self-consciously expose its medium, language, as a function of our fallen legacy, a medium

through which we can never hope to represent or comprehend
divine justice. It will prompt us to search for the true meaning and
origin of God's relation to man yet it will continually remind us
that the narrative upon which such an understanding is founded is
a narrative that is beyond our means of comprehension. So in
leading the reader along blind alleys, in confronting us with
paradoxes and contradictions, Milton, within a Christian context,
anticipated the keynote of deconstruction in Derrida's use of the
term *différance*. The spelling '-ance' instead of '-ence' indicates the
contrast (in French) between 'differing' and 'deferring' and
Derrida's point is that the effect of meaning in language is generated by its difference from alternative meanings, yet at the same
time this meaning must be forever deferred; it will never come to
rest upon a reality, an absolute presence outside language, and
will only move without end through the linguistic system. *Paradise
Lost* reminds us, as Michael puts it, to, hope no higher, because
we are locked into a perceptual and communicative system whose
limits are a reflection of our fallen state. Derrida stated in *Writing
and Difference* that 'the absence of (a presence, or) a transcendental signified (or final pre-linguistic meaning) extends the
domain and play of signification infinitely'. Milton would agree
with this at one level, but he would add that our faith and belief in
the transcendental signified (God) will eventually be rewarded
when we move beyond the imprisonment of our temporal mode,
of which language is a continual reminder. *Paradise Lost* invokes
the transcendental signified, encourages us to search for what
Derrida calls 'the metaphysics of presence' only to confront us
with the origins of our position in the domain of infinite play and
signification – the doubts and anarchic uncertainties of deconstructive method are a consequence of our first misuse of reason
and language. Deconstruction might well be the Tower of Babel in
its modern, secular manifestation.

> each to other calls
> Not understood, still hoarse, and all in rage
> As mocked by storm; great laughter was in heaven
> And looking down, to see the hubbub strange
> And hear the din; thus was the building left
> Ridiculous, and the work Confusion named.
>
> (XII, 57–62)

Would it stretch credibility to read this as a very shrewd anticipation of what would happen to *Paradise Lost* in its journey
through post-seventeenth-century history? True, we could not
argue that Milton offered his poem, perhaps in the manner of

Beckett, as the source of 'hubbub strange' and 'Confusion', but it has certainly been the focus, the catalyst for the seemingly endless 'calls/Not understood' between critics and literary theorists.

The builders of the Tower of Babel thought they might obtain access to the source of absolute certainty and stability by building a tower to heaven. The tower and its appalling, almost farcical consequences is, at least in the Old Testament, a literal fact, but it is also a metaphor for what Derrida calls 'aporia'. Aporia, in a literal translation from the Greek, is the track that leads nowhere, and this phenomenon has been deployed by deconstructionists to show that each text, each claim to truth, will eventually subvert its own grounds and coherence and disperse its apparent meanings into indeterminacy. *Paradise Lost* provokes and incites aporia. No single critical formula will ever account for its interweavings of what we know and recognize and what we will never fully understand. Attempts finally to explain it will result in the same cacophony of voices and proclamations that attended the building of the tower. Milton's 'solution' is to abandon speculation and return to faith, but perhaps he knew that his readers would never, to paraphrase Adam, 'have their fill of knowledge... beyond which was their folly to aspire'. Suspending for a moment any doubts we might have regarding the existence of an afterlife, might we assume that the great laughter in heaven prompted by the building of the tower has been joined by the otherwise sombre voice of John Milton as he observes the progress of his poem?

Summary

Tracing the history of *Paradise Lost* through the writings of poets and critical analysts is rather like discovering new ways of naming what is already present. Christians, humanists, psychoanalysts, Marxists, feminists do not present us with a secret code through which we might finally disentangle the puzzle of the poet and the poem; the puzzle remains unsolved and as it is subjected to each new branch of literary or ideological affiliation it deepens and intensifies. Am I crediting Milton with a level of universality and prescience that is more than he deserves?

In 1988 a volume of commissioned essays on the state of the art in Milton studies was published (*Re-Membering Milton*, eds Nyquist and Ferguson). The final, and by implication the most prominent, essay is by Terry Eagleton, one of the best-known iconoclasts in the new interdisciplinary field of critical theory. In 1983 Eagleton had cited *Paradise Lost*, or rather the study of it, as an example of the privileged status of 'literary studies' in modern society, and argued for its demystification as just another level of socio-cultural awareness.

> The point is whether it is possible to speak of 'literary theory' without perpetuating the illusion that literature exists as a distinct, bounded object of knowledge, or whether it is not preferable to draw the practical consequences of the fact that literary theory can handle Bob Dylan just as well as John Milton.
>
> (*Literary Theory: An Introduction*, p. 204)

But in his 1988 essay called 'The God that Failed' he seems to have changed his opinion, arguing that the poem is a 'historically determined clash of semiotic codes', 'a tormentedly ambiguous historical text which must be laboriously scanned for signs of [Milton's] presence and purpose' – hardly the kind of interpretive conundrums presented by the lyrics of Bob Dylan. At one point he slips almost apologetically into the tradition of interpretation that has attended the poem since its creation. 'If there is a twentieth century candidate for Milton's Satan, it is surely Stalin. Both are overdetermined images of pompous princeling and perverted revolutionary, undecidable amalgams of traditional monarch and power thirsty popular representative' (p. 348). The validity of Eagleton's analogy is less significant that the fact that he concedes, albeit by implication, that the poem maintains the power to create an uncomfortable pattern of identification in the reader. Satan might be Cromwell, Charles I or Stalin but above all he, and his fellow inhabitants of the poem, enact patterns of behaviour that will find correspondences in the reader's confrontation with the most troubling question of the human condition: Why do we behave as we do?

Where Now?

Suggestions for Further Reading will provide starting points for the continued pursuit of Milton through the critical maze, but I shall close this study of his poem with what to me seem useful if slightly unusual recommendations.

In 1989 Raman Selden published a guide to the practical application of the latest interpretive techniques, (*Practising Theory and Interpreting Literature. An Introduction*). He tests each critical category (structuralism, formalism etc.) against a text which will respond fruitfully to its methodology and emphasis. *Paradise Lost* appears in the chapter on Marxist and feminist criticism. Is this a case of natural selection? Does the poem engage with the analytical agenda of the Marxist (class, history and social conflict) and the feminist (gender distinction, the patriarchal domination of the literary canon) more readily that it would with, say, psychoanalysis, formalism or narrative theory? Selden implies that history and sexuality are the points at which *Paradise Lost* intersects with the interpretive agenda of the informed modern reader. What about the Christian reader? 'Christian interpretation' used to be a category that we would find in study guides to, particularly sixteenth- and seventeenth-century, texts, but since the mid-seventies it has been effectively displaced by the more scientific codes within which Christianity, like capitalism or madness, has come to be regarded as an intriguing state of mind, something which was shared by certain writers and certain readers and which contributed to the complex socio-cultural network of signs that the informed reader, like the archaeologist, will judge from a distance. Perhaps this means that we should now despatch the debate between the neo-Satanists (Waldock and Empson) and the Christians (Lewis) to the safe distance of 'before our time', rather as we have with the Romantics? The debate is still alive but we might look outside the clinical protocols of academe for its more engaging manifestations.

It could be argued that Stanley Fish's *Surprised By Sin* (1967) marked the beginning of 'post-Christian' Milton criticism – the 'constructed' rather than embodied Christian and non-Christian approaches. But two years later Kingsley Amis published a very peculiar novel called *The Green Man*. In this, God appears in the twentieth-century sitting room of a drunken, lecherous innkeeper Maurice Allington, whose existence has already been disturbed by a grotesque Satanic agency. Allington asks God why he continues to make life so hard for people (Amis had read Empson's *Milton's God*). God replies:

> 'No prospect of that, I'm afraid. Much too risky from the security point of view. I daren't take the chance of coming that far out into the open. Some of your chaps have found out quite enough already. Your friend Milton'. The young man nodded over at my book shelves. 'He caught on to the idea of the work of art and the game and the rules and so forth. Just as well it never quite dawned on him who Satan was, or rather who he was a piece of. I'd have had to step in there if it had.' (Ch. 4)[8]

This sounds like an intriguing reinterpretation of the poem, but you'll have to look for yourself to see how Allington copes with Adam's legacy. It would seem that the old-fashioned notion of *Paradise Lost* as a shock to the existential system is more deeply felt by modern creative writers than by their academic counterparts. In 1978 D.J. Enright published a collection of poems called

Paradise Illustrated. The sequence follows the narrative of *Paradise Lost*, but the controlling voice is now that of the twentieth-century sceptic who views Milton's characters, like an updated Empson, through the lens of contemporary experience. But the problems raised in 1667 have not gone away. Read the collection for yourself; the following exchange might whet your appetite. We're at Book XII and Michael is showing Adam the future, including, it would seem, the works of John Milton.

XIX   So the Archangel, out of pity,
Now disclosed the liberal arts
That should relieve man's fallen lot.
'Like music, painting, plays and books.'

'Long books?' asked doleful Adam,
Whom the stern Angel had appraised
Of death and rape and guns and hunger.

'A book there'll be,' the Angel said,
'About this very business –
A poem of ten thousand lines, which one
Called Milton shall compose in time to come'.

'Oh dear!' Then Adam brightened.
'Am I the hero of this book perchance?'
'Not quite the hero,' Michael mildly said,
'And yet you feature largely in it –
God, not unnaturally, is the hero.'
'Should have known,' groaned Adam.

'Although there are – or will be – those
Who claim the hero really is – or will be –
Satan. As I of late foretold,
Henceforth the human race is fallible.'

'That circus snake?' hissed Adam scornfully.
Eve hid her blushes in her work,
A garment she was knitting, made with
Real lamb's wool, tight-fitting.

'In my opinion, which I trust
You won't repeat,' the Angel whispered,
'The hero really is the Son,
Called Jesus, even though his lines
Are fewer in the poem that are mine.'

'And me?' Eve raised her eyes. 'Am I in this –
This book of yours? Or, as I well suppose,
Are all the characters men?'

'Indeed you are!' the genial Angel cried,
'Without an Eve there'd be no tale.
While Mr. Milton's not a woman's man,
He does your beauty justice, and your brains'.

'A female intellectual?' Eve grew vexed,
Old-fashioned in her ways as yet.
'No,' spoke the nervous Angel, blushing more,
'I only meant, not just a pretty face'.

Eve held the knitting to her breast.
'By me the Promised Seed shall all restore.'
And Michael knew the time was ripe to leave.
'All – or some,' he murmured at the door.[9]

Notes

Chapter 2 – Openings: Books I–IV

1 The debate that attended Milton's use of blank verse in a non-dramatic poem is comparable with that caused by free verse in this century. For a more detailed account see R.D. Haven's *The Influence of Milton on English Poetry* (1922) and Richard Bradford's *Silence and Sound. Theories of Poetics from the Eighteenth Century* (1992).

2 Christopher Ricks in *Milton's Grand Style* (1963) draws extensively upon eighteenth-century critics and editors of the poem.

3 There is a vast number of theoretical studies of metaphor, but Terence Hawkes's 'Critical Idiom' guide, *Metaphor* (1972) is the most accessible. See also S. Sacks (ed.) *On Metaphor* (1979) and C. Brooke-Rose, *A Grammar of Metaphor* (1958).

4 New Historicism can be defined in a number of ways, but in this instance it means the examination of literary texts not merely as aesthetic artefacts but as components of a broader network of media (sermons, pamphlets, popular myths) that contribute to the consciousness of a particular age. Fish is also regarded as a proponent of reader-response criticism in that he regards the beliefs and prejudices of a particular 'interpretive community' to be as significant as the intended meaning of a text.

Chapter 3 – The Fall: Books V–IX

1 On fire and the Fall see also V, 349; IX, 397–2 and X, 1078–81, and refer to Alastair Fowler's notes on these passages.

2 A chronology of criticism would be useful here. A.J.A. Waldock (1947) is regarded as the first modern, academic counterpart to the Romantic pro-Satanists. To him, Milton's God was so nasty that Satan's revolt against divine tyranny must seem reasonable and justified. Empson (1961) picked up where Waldock left off, and conducted a thorough re-reading of the poem based upon the assumption that Milton intended to present God as a capricious sadist. The modern critic with whom they both take issue is C.S. Lewis (*A Preface to Paradise Lost*, 1942).

3 Sutton's *Lectures Upon the Eleventh Chapter to the Romans* (1632)

have not been reprinted. This passage is from pp. 460–1, and is also referred to by Stanley Fish in *Surprised By Sin* pp. 244–5.

4 See M. Landy, 'Kinship and the Role of Women in *Paradise Lost*', *Milton Studies* 4 (1972), pp. 3–18 and '"A Free and Open Encounter": Milton and the Modern Reader', *Milton Studies* 9 (1976), pp. 3–36. B.K. Lewalski, 'Milton on Women – Yet Once More', *Milton Studies* 6 (1974), pp. 3–20. Feminist criticism is dealt with more fully in Chapter 5.

5 The best selection of metaphysical verse is Helen Gardner's edition for Penguin (1957), which also contains a useful introduction to the genre. T.S. Eliot's seminal essay 'The Metaphysical Poets' (1921) will be looked at in Chapters 4 and 5.

6 For a detailed study of Milton's familiarity with contemporary astronomy see Grant McColley, 'Milton's Dialogue on Astronomy', *PMLA* 1ii (1937), pp. 728–62.

7 Alastair Fowler provides a useful note on Pliny and the gnostics on p. 405 of his edition of the poem.

Chapter 4 – Outcomes and Consequences: Books X–XII

1 A.O. Lovejoy's 'Milton and the Paradox of the Fortunate Fall' (first published 1945) will be found in C.A. Patrides's collection *Milton's Epic Poetry. Essays on Paradise Lost and Paradise Regained* (1967).

2 Eliot's essay was first published in 1921. You will find a reprint in his *Selected Essays* (1961). The quotations here and in Chapter 5 are taken from *The Oxford Anthology of English Literature* Vol. II, p. 2024.

Chapter 5 – Criticism

1 A selection of eighteenth-century criticism of *Paradise Lost*, including Dryden, Pope, Addison and Johnson, will be found in A.E. Dyson's and Julian Lovelock's selection *Milton: Paradise Lost* (Macmillan casebook series 1973).

2 These quotes are taken from the Dyson and Lovelock collection – see n. 1 above.

3 See F.R. Leavis's *Revaluation* (1936), pp. 42–61. Eliot's essays on Milton were first published in 1936 and 1947 and reprinted in *On Poetry and Poets* (1957). These quotes are from the Dyson and Lovelock collection, pp. 80, 77.

4 *Oxford Anthology of English Literature*, Vol. II, p. 2025.

5 For a guide to the roots of structuralism in linguistics and anthropology see Terence Hawkes's *Structuralism and Semiotics* (1977).

6 K.M. Rogers' *The Troublesome Helpmate* (1966) is based more on objective biblical scholarship than feminist theory. Compare this with Diane McColley's *Milton's Eve* (1983), which employs the methodology of more than a decade's work in feminist criticism.

7 See Geoffrey Hartman, 'Adam on the Grass with Balsamum', *Beyond Formalism* (1970), pp. 124–50. Mary Nyquist, 'Reading the Fall:

Discourse in Drama in *Paradise Lost*'. *English Literary Renaissance* 14 (1984), pp. 199–229.

8 *The Green Man* (1969) is now in paperback with Penguin. See also Richard Bradford's *Kingsley Amis* (1989), pp. 54–60.

9 This appears in Enright's *Collected Poems* (1981), pp. 155–77.

Suggestions for Further Reading

The critics already cited offer an accurate reflection of the poem's effect on twentieth-century critical thinking, with centre stage being held by the Christian–non Christian debate between Lewis, Waldock, Empson and Fish. In what follows I shall suggest entry points to these and other debates, and a good place to start would be with studies of the historical context.

History

Christopher Hill's *Milton and the English Revolution* (1977) has already been discussed and in my view it is the most detailed yet accessible survey of the society and system of political and religious beliefs inhabited by Milton and his contemporaries. Hill's Marxist approach is challenged by S. Davies in *Images of Kingship in Paradise Lost* (1983) who claims that the political resonances of the poem draw more upon theoretical, abstract notions of leadership than upon contemporary events, and by A. Milner in *John Milton and the English Revolution* (1981) who claims that Hill is insufficiently rigorous in his application of Marxist critical technique – Milner shifts towards the interpretive model of context determining content. M. Ross's *Milton and Royalism* (1943) is one of the first and most accessible modern studies of the Satan–God–Charles I–Cromwell conundrum.

Biography

The most recent and in my view the most engaging biography is *The Life of John Milton* by A.N. Wilson (1983). Wilson goes against the 'over theorizing' of the academic historians and critics (Hill and Empson) and presents us with a vivid picture of the man and his writings. For those who wish to go deeper into fact and detail, start with W.R. Parker's *Milton. A Biography* (1968), move on to Helen Darbishire's edition of

The Early Lives of John Milton (1932) and end with the monumental *Life of Milton* by David Masson (1859–80, 7 vols). The shortest, most accessible and pleasantly illustrated biography is C.V. Wedgwood's *Milton and His World* (1969).

Style and Form

The best book on Milton's style is Christopher Ricks's *Milton's Grand Style* (1963). Once you've read Ricks you begin to notice that the vast novelistic scope is actually assembled from short and intriguingly difficult poetic devices. His opening chapter is a skilful savaging of such sceptics as Johnson, Eliot and Leavis. Arnold Stein's *Answerable Style: Essays on Paradise Lost* (1953) predates Ricks as a modern revaluation of Milton's techniques but Stein lacks Ricks's interpretive panache. For those who wish to consider the effect of Paradise Lost's stylistic innovations on eighteenth- and nineteenth-century English poets R.D. Haven's *The Influence of Milton on English Poetry* (1922) is the book to consult. For scholarly accounts of grammar, diction and prosody, see R.D. Emma's *Milton's Grammar* (1964), F.T. Prince's *The Italian Element in Milton's Verse* (1954) and S.E. Sprott's *Milton's Art of Prosody* (1953). Richard Bradford's *Silence and Sound. Theories of Poetics from the Eighteenth Century* (1992) shows how *Paradise Lost* anticipates elements of modernist technique.

Critical Schools and Critical History

The journey of *Paradise Lost* through the different schools and affiliations of modern critical theory has already been charted in Chapter 5. To continue to test your own perceptions of the poem against the ever-changing moods and methods of the critical world you could begin by consulting Margerita Stocker's *Paradise Lost* ('The Critics Debate' series 1988). Stocker divides modern critics into categories such as 'Psychology and Myth', 'Feminist', 'Historical' etc., and her bibliography is reliable and comprehensive. But where do you begin? The best way to appreciate how opinions on the same issues can change with time and circumstances is to conduct a compare and contrast exercise. Feminism for example; have a look at Robert Graves's satirical novel on Milton's marriage (*Wife to Mr. Milton* 1942) and E.M.W. Tillyard's discussion of Milton's relations with women in his critical biography from the same period (*Milton* 1930), and then turn to a more recent feminist reading of the man, his life, and his work in Diane McColley's *Milton's Eve* (1983). The facts and the characters are the same but their effect upon perceptions of how men relate to and write about women have changed radically. To broaden the range of this exercise you could first consult two much recommended collections, Frank Kermode's *The Living Milton* (1960) and C.A. Patrides's *Milton's Epic Poetry* (1967). These catch the mood of how contemporary (1960s) critics such as Empson and Ricks had set about rescuing the 'living Milton' from the scepticism of the 1920s and 1930s (see Leavis and Eliot). Then move on a quarter of a century to *Re-Membering Milton. Essays on the Texts and Traditions* (ed. M.

Nyquist and M. Ferguson 1988). This collection shows that the debate has changed from whether or not Milton was a great writer to how he engages with more recent interdisciplinary concerns – literature and gender, literature and post-Marxist theory, literature and oppression, literature and the academic establishment. A reasonably accessible reading of the encounter between Milton and new interpretive theory occurs in Catherine Belsey's *John Milton. Language, Gender and Power* (1989), but you might also find that this study is an instance of the effect we considered at the end of Chapter 5 – the systems, techniques and affiliations of the interpreter have overshadowed and overridden the individuality of the poet.

You will find a short selection of pre-twentieth-century criticism in Dyson and Lovelock's *Paradise Lost. A Selection of Critical Essays* (Macmillan 'casebook' series 1973) and a more comprehensive one in J.T. Shawcross's *Milton: The Critical Heritage* (1970).

Bibliography

Addison, Joseph. *The Spectator.* Ed. D.F. Bond, 5 vols (Oxford, Oxford University Press 1965).
Amis, Kingsley. *The Green Man* (London, Cape 1969).
Belsey, C. *John Milton. Language, Gender and Power* (Oxford, Blackwell 1989).
Bennett, J.S. 'God, Satan, and King Charles: Milton's Royal Portraits', *PMLA* 92 (1977), pp. 441–57.
Blake, William. *The Marriage of Heaven and Hell* (1790). Reprinted in Dyson and Lovelock, p. 44.
Bloom, Harold. *The Anxiety of Influence* (New York and London, Oxford University Press 1973).
Bradford, Richard. *Kingsley Amis* (London, Edward Arnold 1989).
Bradford, Richard. *Silence and Sound. Theories of Poetics from the Eighteenth Century* (New Jersey and London, Associated University Presses 1992).
Brooke-Rose, Christine. *A Grammar of Metaphor* (London, Secker & Warburg 1958).
Cormican, L.A. 'Milton's Religious Verse', in *The Penguin Guide to English Literature, III, From Donne to Marvell.* Ed. Boris Ford (London, Penguin 1960).
Darbishire, Helen (ed.). *The Early Lives of John Milton* (London, Constable 1932).
Davies, S. *Images of Kinship in Paradise Lost* (Columbia, Miss., Missouri University Press 1983).
Derrida, Jacques. *Writing and Difference* (Chicago, Chicago University Press 1978).
Dyson, A.E. and Lovelock Julian. *Milton: Paradise Lost. A Selection of Critical Essays* (London, Macmillan 1973).
Eagleton, Terry. *Literary Theory: An Introduction* (Oxford, Blackwell 1983).
Eagleton, Terry. 'The God That Failed' in *Re-Membering Milton.* Eds M. Nyquist and M. Ferguson (London, Methuen 1988).
Eliot, T.S. 'The Metaphysical Poets' (1921). Reprinted in *Selected Essays* (London, Faber 1961).
Eliot, T.S. 'Milton I' (1936); 'Milton II' (1947). Reprinted in *On Poetry and Poets* (London, Faber 1957).

Emma, R.D. *Milton's Grammar* (The Hague, Mouton 1964).

Empson, William. *Milton's God* (London, Chatto & Windus 1961).

Enright, D.J. *Collected Poems* (Oxford, Oxford University Press 1981).

Fallon, R.T. *Captain or Colonel* (Columbia, Miss., Missouri University Press 1984).

Fish, Stanley. *Surprised By Sin: The Reader in Paradise Lost* (New York and London, St Martins Press and Macmillan 1967).

Freud, Sigmund. 'Creative Writers and Day-Dreaming', in *Twentieth Century Literary Criticism*. Ed. David Lodge (London, Longmans 1972).

Gardner, Helen (ed.). *The Metaphysical Poets* (London, Penguin 1957).

Gilbert, S. 'Patriarchal Poetry and Women Readers: Reflections on Milton's Bogey', *PMLA* 93 (1978), pp. 368–82.

Graves, R. *Wife to Mr. Milton* (London, Cassell 1942).

Hartman, G. 'Adam on the Grass with Balsamum', in *Beyond Formalism* (New Haven and London, Yale University Press 1970).

Havens, R.D. *The Influence of Milton on English Poetry* (Cambridge, Mass., Harvard University Press 1922).

Hawkes, Terence. *Metaphor* (London, Methuen 1972).

Hawkes, Terence. *Structuralism and Semiotics* (London, Methuen 1977).

Hill, Christopher. *Milton and The English Revolution* (London, Faber 1977).

Johnson, Samuel. 'Milton', in *The Lives of the English Poets* (1779). Reprinted in Dyson and Lovelock, pp. 40–3.

Kermode, Frank (ed.). *The Living Milton* (London, Routledge & Kegan Paul 1960).

Kerrigan, W. *The Prophetic Milton* (Charlottesville, Virginia University Press 1974).

Kerrigan, W. *The Sacred Complex* (Cambridge, Mass. and London, Harvard University Press 1983).

Landy, M. 'Kinship and the Role of Women in *Paradise Lost*', *Milton Studies* 4 (1972), pp. 3–18.

Landy, M. '"A Free and Open Encounter": Milton and the Modern Reader', *Milton Studies* 9 (1976), pp. 3–36.

Leavis, F.R. *Revaluation* (London, Chatto & Windus 1936).

Lewalski, B.K. 'Milton on Women – Yet Once More', *Milton Studies* 6 (1974), pp. 3–20.

Lewis, C.S. *A Preface to Paradise Lost* (Oxford, Oxford University Press 1942).

McColley, Diane K. *Milton's Eve* (Champaign, Illinois University Press 1983).

McColley, Grant. 'Milton's Dialogue on Astronomy' *PMLA* 1ii (1937), pp. 728–62.

Masson, David. *Life of Milton*, 7 vols. (London, 1859–80).

Milner, A. *John Milton and the English Revolution* (London, Macmillan 1981).

Milton, John. *Paradise Lost*. Ed. Alastair Fowler (London, Longmans 1968).

Milton, John. *Complete Shorter Poems*. Ed. John Carey (London, Longmans 1968).

Milton, John. *Complete Prose Works* (Yale, Yale University Press 1953).

Muir, Kenneth. *Milton.* (London, Longmans 1955).

Nyquist, M. 'Reading The Fall: Discourse in Drama in *Paradise Lost*', *English Literary Renaissance* 14 (1984), pp. 199–229.

Nyquist, M. and Ferguson, M. (eds). *Re-Membering Milton. Essays on the Texts and Traditions* (New York and London, Methuen 1988).

Parker, W.R. *Milton. A Biography* (Oxford, Oxford University Press 1968).

Patrides, C.A. (ed.). *Milton's Epic Poetry. Essays on Paradise Lost and Paradise Regained* (London, Penguin 1967).

Prince, F.T. *The Italian Element in Milton's Verse* (Oxford, Clarendon 1954).

Revard, S.P. *The War In Heaven* (Ithaca, NY and London, Cornell University Press 1980).

Ricks, C. *Milton's Grand Style* (Oxford, Oxford University Press 1963).

Rogers, K.M. *The Troublesome Helpmate* (Seattle and London, Washington University Press 1966).

Ross, M. *Milton and Royalism* (Ithaca, NY, Cornell University Press 1943).

Sacks, S. (ed.). *On Metaphor* (Chicago, Chicago University Press 1979).

Selden, R. *Practising Theory and Reading Literature. An Introduction* (London, Harvester Wheatsheaf 1989).

Shawcross, J.T. (ed.). *Milton: The Critical Heritage* (London, Routledge 1970).

Sprott, S.E. *Milton's Art of Prosody* (Oxford, Blackwell 1953).

Stein, A. *Answerable Style: Essays on Paradise Lost* (Minneapolis and London, University of Minnesota Press 1953).

Stocker, M. *Paradise Lost.* The Critics Debate Series (London, Macmillan 1988).

Tillyard, E.M.W. *Milton* (London, Chatto & Windus 1930).

Waldock, A.J.A. *Paradise Lost and Its Critics* (Cambridge, Cambridge University Press 1947).

Webber, J.M. 'The Politics of Poetry: Feminism and *Paradise Lost*', *Milton Studies* 14 (1980), pp. 3–24.

Wedgwood, C.V. *Milton and His World* (London, Lutterworth Press 1969).

Whiting, G.W. *Milton's Literary Milieu* (New York, Russell & Russell 1964).

Wilson, A.N. *The Life of John Milton* (Oxford, Oxford University Press 1983).

Index